Maine

Coastal Cooking

and the

Accomplifht Cook,

O R,

The whole Art and Myftery of
C O O K E R Y, fitted for all Degrees and Qualities.

Down East recipes dating from 1664

DOWN
EAST BOOKS   CAMDEN/MAINE

ISBN-089272-094-8

A Down East Book

Camden, Maine 04843

Printed in the United States of America

Maine Coastal Cooking

Good cooks are many along the coast of Maine. We selected two of the best to bring together the recipes which are contained within Coastal Cooking, Mrs. Ruth Wiggin of Rockland and Mrs. Gertrude Hupper of Martinsville.

Both Mrs. Wiggin and Mrs. Hupper have had long years of experience in the work of the Knox-Lincoln Extension Association in the homemaking and foods fields. Their work has also extended into the directing of 4-H Clubs in the Coastal Area of Maine.

Countless good cooks along the shore have contributed their favorite recipes to these two foods experts for inclusion in Coastal Cooking. Some of the recipes date back a century or more. Many have been handed down through the generations of Maine coast families with no one knowing actually how far back into history they date. It is a certainty that many came from Colonial days and even back to pioneer days when Maine was a wilderness in the process of being settled along the coast by hardy pioneers from the westward.

Several are reprinted from the newspaper files of The Courier-Gazette at Rockland, Maine which has been in continuous publication since 1846.

The final 24 pages of Coastal Cooking takes one back to 1664 in what is now Massachusetts, and even back to England. The recipes contained there are taken from "The Accomplished Cook: or, The Art and Mystery of Cookery." This rare and valuable cookbook, perhaps one of the first to be printed, was loaned by Mr. Ralph W. Bartlett of Bremen, Maine whose forebears came into possession of it upwards of 300 years ago.

Index of recipes follows page 66.

Boiled Maine Lobster

Place the live lobsters in a kettle containing about three inches of briskly boiling salted water. Cover immediately. From time water boils again, allow 18 to 20 minutes. Serve whole lobster, either hot or cold, with a side dish of melted butter or use lemon sauce.

LEMON SAUCE

4 tablespoons butter, melted   1 teaspoon lemon juice
⅛ teaspoon pepper
Blend together, serve hot over lobster meat.

Maine Lobster Stew

For each full serving or bowl, allow the meat from one chicken lobster. After lobsters have been boiled remove meat immediately, saving the tomalley and coral if desired. For four servings, simmer the tomalley and coral in one-half cup butter 7 or 8 minutes, using a heavy kettle. Add the lobster meat, cut in fairly large pieces and cook 10 minutes over low heat. Remove from heat and cool slightly. Add very slowly, one quart rich hot milk, stirring constantly. Use salt and pepper to taste. Allow the stew to stand 5 or 6 hours before reheating for serving. This is one of the secrets of truly fine flavor. When cooling stew, do not cover until thoroughly cold or stew will curdle.

Broiled State of Maine Lobster

4 lobsters (alive)   ½ cup butter   Paprika

Split four Maine lobsters, using a sharp pointed knife, from head to tail. Open lobster flat. Remove intestinal vein, stomach and liver (tomalley). Crack claws.

Baste lobster meat with melted butter. Place on broiler and broil 15 minutes, basting meat with butter frequently until it loosens in the shell.

Remove from oven and sprinkle each lobster with a little paprika. Serve with melted butter or lemon sauce.

Lobster Croquettes with Sauce Pimiento

4 tablespoons butter	Few grains of salt and pepper
4 tablespoons flour	1 teaspoon lemon juice
1 cup milk	2 cups chopped lobster meat

Prepare white sauce by adding flour to melted butter, then add to hot milk and cook until it thickens. Season with salt and pepper and add lemon juice and the lobster meat. Chill, roll a heaping tablespoonful of the mixture with the hand, then shape on a board into mounds. Roll in dried bread crumbs, dip into an egg mixture (two tablespoons of water allowed to each beaten egg used) and roll again in crumbs.

Heat deep fat to 390°F. Arrange croquettes in a frying basket, a few at a time, and lower into the fat and fry until delicately browned. Serve hot with Sauce Pimiento.

SAUCE PIMIENTO

Prepare one cup and one-half of white sauce made by using one cup of milk, one-half cup of cream, three tablespoons each of butter and flour, and seasoning of salt and pepper. Add one-half cup of chopped pimiento.

Lobster Cocktail

Allow 2 cups fresh cooked lobster meat, cut in pieces for six servings; arrange in cocktail glasses and top with cocktail sauce.

COCKTAIL SAUCE

(Large Recipe)

1 pint catsup	Few grains of salt
1 tablespoon horseradish	Paprika
1 tablespoon vinegar	2 drops tobasco sauce
1½ teaspoons Worcestershire sauce	

Simmer together for 20 minutes.

4

Lobster Pie

2 tablespoons butter
¼ cup sherry
1 cup well-packed lobster meat
¾ cup thin cream

3 tablespoons butter
1 tablespoon flour
2 egg yolks

Add sherry to 2 tablespoons melted butter; boil one minute. Add lobster and let stand. Melt 3 tablespoons butter; add flour and stir until it bubbles 1 minute. Remove from heat; slowly stir in cream and wine drained from lobster. Return to heat and cook, stirring constantly until sauce is smooth and thick. Remove from heat.

Heat the sauce in top of a double boiler over hot but not boiling water. (The sauce may curdle if the water boils.) Stir constantly while heating, about 3 minutes. Remove from heat; add lobster. Turn into small deep pie plate. Sprinkle with topping and bake in 300 degree oven for 10 minutes.

TOPPING

Mix ¼ cup cracker meal, ¼ teaspoon paprika, 1 tablespoon finely crushed potato chips and 1½ tablespoons Parmesan cheese. Add 2 tablespoons melted butter and blend well.

Submitted by Mrs. Richard D. Spring, Rockland, Maine

Baked Stuffed Lobster

4 lobsters (alive)
1½ cups cracker crumbs
½ teaspoon salt

4 tablespoons butter (melted)
2 tablespoons hot water

Select 4 lobsters of one size. Split with a sharp pointed knife from head to tail. Open lobster flat. Remove intestinal vein, stomach and liver (tomalley). If you wish, save tomalley for adding to dressing. Crack claws.

Prepare dressing by moistening crumbs with melted butter and hot water, add salt and liver.

Spread dressing generously in cavity and split of tail. Bake on cookie sheet in 450° oven for 20 minutes or until meat is loose in shell.

Maine Lobster Chowder

2 cups lobster meat
4 tablespoons butter
1 cup water
2 cups hot milk

2 cups diced raw potatoes
1 small onion, sliced
Paprika
Salt and pepper

Simmer the lobster meat in the butter over low heat for 7 or 8 minutes.

Combine potatoes, onion, and water and boil until tender. Add hot milk and lobster mixture. Season to taste and add a dash of paprika.

Maine Lobster Salad

For each cup of boiled and chilled lobster meat cut in small pieces, allow one tablespoon mayonnaise, salt and pepper. Mix thoroughly and chill again. Place on crisp lettuce leaves and sprinkle with paprika. Top with a whole lobster claw removed from the shell.

VARIATIONS
1. Add one stalk of celery, diced.
2. Add equal amount of whipped cream to mayonnaise and one-half teaspoon of sugar

Bar Harbor Salad

8 medium sized boiled cold potatoes
2 cups cooked lobster meat   Mayonnaise.
3 tablespoons chopped dill pickle

Dice potato, add enough mayonnaise to hold potatoes together Add lobster and pickle, add more mayonnaise. Serve in lettuce cups garnished with parsley and sliced olives.

Submitted by Mrs. Marion Thayer, RFD 1, Thomaston

Scalloped Lobster

Line the bottom of a pudding dish with cracker or stale bread crumbs; then put in a layer of lobsters seasoned with salt, pepper and

6

butter, and so on until the dish is full, having the top layer of crumbs. Lay small lumps of butter over the top, pour over half a pint of cream; set it in the oven and bake half an hour. Serve at once.

Maine Lobster Newburg

2 cups lobster meat, boiled and diced
1 cup cream or whole milk — ¼ teaspoon salt
2 egg yolks, beaten — 4 tablespoons melted butter
1 tablespoon flour — Paprika
1 teaspoon lemon juice or vinegar

Heat the lobster in 3 tablespoons melted butter, do not brown. In another saucepan, stir flour well into other tablespoon of butter, add cream, heat, stir well, until smooth. When boiling starts remove from heat and add egg yolks and stir until thick.

Add heated lobster and lemon juice, do not heat again as it may curdle. Serve on toasted crackers or toast.

Creamed Crabmeat on Waffles

Crabmeat (1 cup - fresh or canned)
2 tablespoons shortening — 3 eggs
2 tablespoons flour — ½ teaspoon salt
½ teaspoon salt — 3 tablespoons salad oil
1 cup milk — 1 cup light cream
Few grains of pepper — 1½ cups cake flour
1 teaspoon butter — 2 teaspoons baking powder

Flake crabmeat and fold into the white sauce.

SAUCE

Rub to a smooth paste, the melted shortening, flour and salt; add milk and pepper, stir and cook until thickened. Add butter for seasoning, but avoid seasonings which would cover up the delicate flavor of the crabmeat. Serve piping hot on freshly baked waffles.

CREAM WAFFLES

Beat eggs, add salt, salad oil, one-half a cup of light cream, then the cake flour. Mix to a smooth, thin batter, cover with waxpaper, refrigerate until ready to use, then add baking powder, sifted, and mix well.

Use about 3 large mixing spoons of batter for each waffle. Bake in heated waffle iron about 2½ minutes or until done. Serve immediately.

Midget Cheese Puffs with Crab Salad

1 cup water	½ teaspoon salt
½ cup butter	4 eggs
1 cup flour	½ cup grated cheese

In a saucepan, place the water and butter and heat to the boiling point. Add the flour and salt all at once and stir vigorously until the mixture is well blended and smooth. Remove from the heat and add the unbeaten eggs one at a time, stirring after each addition to incorporate them thoroughly. Fold in the grated cheese. Drop by teaspoon on an oiled baking sheet and bake at 425°F. for the first ten minutes, then reduce the heat to 375°F. and continue cooking about 20 minutes more. Cool. Gash along one side and fill with crab salad.

Crab Stew

2 tablespoons butter	6 small soda crackers
2 cups fresh crabmeat (1 can)	½ cup water (hot or cold)

Melt butter slowly in kettle, add crabmeat, finely crushed crackers and water — stir well and let boil for 1 minute. Add 1 quart milk, ½ teaspoon salt, ½ teaspoon accent, and a shaking of paprika. Stir as it heats, then add 1 can of evaporated milk or 1 cup of cream.

Crab Newburg

2 cups crabmeat
4 tablespoons butter   ½ teaspoon salt
3 tablespoons flour   Few grains pepper
½ cup boiling water or hot milk

Melt butter, add flour, salt and pepper, slowly add hot water
or milk to make thick sauce. Then add 1 pint thin cream and
stir in as you add 2 cups crabmeat and a dash of nutmeg. Stir until
well heated through. Just before serving add ¼ to ½ cup of sherry.
Serve on toast points or saltines. Serves 4.

Crab and Tomato Salad

1 cup crabmeat   2/3 cup celery   6 tomatoes
Remove meat from hard-shelled crabs. Add celery, cut in small
pieces, and tomatoes peeled, chilled and cut in quarters. Moisten with
mayonnaise. Serve on lettuce leaves and garnish with mayonnaise and
curled celery.

Shrimp Salad

1 pound cooked shrimp, diced   Mayonnaise
2 cups finely minced celery   Lettuce
Juice of 1 lemon   Pimiento strips
Salt and paprika

Mix shrimp, celery, mayonnaise, lemon juice and seasoning.
Clean the lettuce and arrange 6 nests about 4 inches across. Use a
small cup as a mold, fill with the shrimp mixture and press firm; invert
the molded contents into each lettuce nest. Add a teaspoon of mayonnaise and paprika or crossed strips of pimiento. If desired, the celery
may be omitted and replaced by cloves, capers, etc.

How To Cook Shrimp

Shrimp should be boiled as follows — Wash the shrimp thoroughly, cover with boiling salted water (½ tablespoon per quart) and
simmer 15-20 minutes until tender and pink. Drain. Tear each

shell open from underside, from head toward tail, and with a sharp-pointed knife, remove the black cord visible just under the surface. Shrimp may now be used for serving in accordance with various recipes.

Shrimp Hobby Horses

Select extremely large olives stuffed with pimientos, and large shrimp, either canned or fresh. Remove the dark streak from each shrimp with a sharpened knife. Wrap the olives and the shrimps with short pieces of bacon and skewer with toothpicks. Place under broiler to brown; turn and brown on other side. Serve sizzling hot, with crisp wafers or tiny hot biscuits. Arrange the hobby horses on an hors d'oeuvre holder set upon a wooden tray with wafers or biscuits circling it.

Asparagus and Shrimps in Aspic

2 tablespoons plain granulated gelatine

1 cup cold water	1/3 cup additional cold water
4 bouillon cubes	Whale shrimps
2 cups boiling water	Green asparagus tips
¼ cup lemon juice	Olives

Let gelatine dissolve in cold water. Dissolve bouillon cubes in boiling water, add to gelatine and stir until dissolved; let cool, add lemon juice and water, pour enough of this liquid onto a serving tray or glass baking dish barely to cover the bottom. To help jell more quickly place tray on a bed of cracked ice and when the gelatine is slightly jellied, so that pieces of food will be held in place, arrange them as desired.

When firm, add a small amount of the liquid gelatine mixture, let chill, then finish covering the arranged foods.

Serve this jellied entree extremely cold with salad dressing or mayonnaise.

Baked Shrimp with Stuffing

Cut shrimps most way through back to devein and lay flat (like a butterfly). Arrange on a shallow baking dish not touching. Drop a generous spoonful of dressing on each shrimp, put on another shrimp and finish with a spoonful of dressing. Pin with toothpicks, add a dab of butter. These may also be broiled single with dressing on top.

Stuffing: 2 cups broken bread, 2 tablespoons minced onion, 2 tablespoons butter, 1 teaspoon parsley, ¼ teaspoon salt, ¼ teaspoon sage, and ⅛ teaspoon pepper. Soak bread, press out water, brown onion in butter, and add with seasoning to crumbs.

Shrimp Saute

¼ cup butter   ½ teaspoon salt
1 minced clove garlic   1 teaspoon accent
1½ pound deveined, shelled medium shrimp
Pepper   1/3 cup snipped parsley

In large skillet, melt butter. Add garlic, salt and accent; saute until garlic is brown. Add shrimp; saute until shrimp are pink on underside; turn; saute until pink on other side. Sprinkle with pepper. Add parsley; cook 1 minute. Serve with lemon juice.

Baked Mussels

Scrub mussels. Open shells with knife like clams. Remove beard. Lay mussels in baking pan. Sprinkle with salt, pepper and chopped onion. Lay strips of bacon on top. Sprinkle with grated cheese. Bake in slow oven (300°) until bacon is crisp. Allow 8 mussels per serving.

Oyster Stew

1 quart oysters   ½ tablespoon salt
¼ cup butter   ⅛ teaspoon pepper
4 cups scalded milk

Clean oysters by placing in a calander and pouring over them ¾ cup cold water. Carefully pick over oysters, reserve liquor, and heat it to boiling point; strain through double cheesecloth, add oysters, and cook until oysters are plump and edges begin to curl. Remove oysters with skimmer and place in a bowl with butter, salt, and pepper. Strain oyster liquor a second time. Return oysters and seasonings to kettle, add strained oyster liquor and scalded milk. Serve with oyster crackers.

February Oysters

2 tablespoons butter
½ cup rice
1½ tablespoons Curry powder

2 cups tomato juice
Few grains of salt
2 dozen oysters

Melt two tablespoonfuls of butter and in it fry ½ cup of rice until it is tinged yellow. Add 2 cups of tomato juice, a little salt and a bit of bay leaf. Simmer for ½ hour. Mix to a paste 1½ tablespoons Curry powder with a little cold tomato juice and stir into the mixture. When smooth, add two dozen oysters, well drained and cook until the oysters begin to curl around the edges. Serve very hot.

Mother's Clam Pudding

Chop one quart clams. Put in casserole with two medium potatoes and two onions sliced thin. Season with salt and pepper. Cover with clam broth and dot with butter.

Roll out rich biscuit dough and cover. Bake in oven starting at 450 degrees until potatoes are done (about 30 minutes). Lower temperature after it begins to bubble.

Dough: 2 cups flour, 2 tablespoons shortening, 1 teaspoon cream of tartar, ½ teaspoon soda, 1 teaspoon salt. Add milk to handle.

Submitted by Mrs. Inga J. Chase, RFD 1, Rockland, Maine

Fried Clams

2 cups flour
½ teaspoon salt, pepper and paprika
1 cup milk
½ cup clam liquor
A little grated onion added to the batter

4 teaspoons baking powder

2 well beaten eggs

Dip each clam in batter and fry in deep fat . They will brown nicely if you use Crisco.

This is a family recipe and the best one I have ever used.

Submitted by Mrs. Edna Dyer, North Haven, Maine

Trudy's Maine Clambake

6 dozen clams (steaming size)   6 potatoes (baking size)
6 white onions
6 ears of yellow sweet corn (in husks)
6 live chicken lobsters

Wash clam shells thoroughly. Wash potatoes. Peel onions. Remove corn from husks and take off silk and knot ends. Rewrap in husks to roast. In an 18 inch strip of freezer type foil wrap 1 dozen clams, a potato, an onion, an ear of corn and 1 lobster in the center — sprinkle wth 1 cup of water and seal tightly by bringing edges of paper together and folding. Roast in seaweed 2 hours.

Prepare fire: Build fire on several large rocks and let burn down to coals, then cover with wet seaweed about 6 inches — lay packages of food on seaweed in single layer. Cover with more seaweed and with an old canvas sail or clean grain bags to keep in steam. Remove cloth after one hour and try potatoes in next half hour, when done serve a package to each person.

Deep Dish Clam Pie

For a family of from 4 to 6 use about 1 quart of shucked clams. Free the clams of sediment. Use a good-sized baking dish or 2 quart casserole. Place a layer of thinly sliced raw potatoes in the dish, and over this a layer of whole clams. Season lightly with salt and pepper. Continue the alternate layers until the dish is nearly full with potatoes on top. Pour in enough milk to come to just the top of the potatoes. Cover with ordinary pie crust. Slit to allow escape of steam. Cook in a moderate oven until top crust is well browned.

My grandmother inverted an old cup in the middle of the pie before putting on the top crust, but I make it without doing so. For myself, if I am in a hurry, I use a small casserole and a small can of minced clams, but I think it tastes better made with the raw clams.

Submitted by Marguerite Gould, Rockland, Maine

Steamed Clams

Clams for steaming should be bought in the shell and always alive. Wash clams thoroughly, scrubbing with a brush, changing the

13

water several times. Put into a large kettle, allowing one-half cup hot water to four quarts clams; cover closely, and steam until shells partially open, care being taken that they are not overdone. The old fashioned rule for steaming is to let the claims boil up and lift up the cover three times then they are done. Save clam liquor as it is delicious to drink. Liquor should be strained and clear.

Serve with individual dishes of melted butter. Some prefer a few drops of lemon juice or vinegar added to the butter. Also serve clam liquor with the clams.

Scalloped Clams

1 can minced clams, juice and all
1 cup cracker crumbs (crushed saltines or Ritz)
1 cup milk   Salt and pepper to taste
¼ cup melted butter or oleo   1 egg beaten

Mix together and let stand about 30 minutes. Bake, in buttered casserole, 45 minutes at 350°.

Clam Stew

1 pint clams   ½ teaspoon salt   Paprika
1 quart whole milk
2 tablespoons butter and 2 tablespoons later

Grind clams in food chopper — save liquor. In a heavy aluminum saucepan heat butter, milk and ½ cup clam liquor, when hot add clams and heat again — just before serving add salt, 2 tablespoons butter and paprika. Serves 4.

Maine Clam Chowder

1 quart of fresh Maine clams   1 quart rich milk, scalded
¼ pound salt pork   Salt and pepper to taste
1 quart diced potatoes   Butter, if desired
1 onion, chopped

Remove black parts from clams, saving the liquor. Cut pork in small pieces and fry until crisp and golden brown, then remove small pieces of pork from the fat. Add potatoes and onion, with just enough hot water to be seen through the potatoes. Cook over low heat—just simmering—until done.

Finally, add clams and cook 2 minutes after coming to a boil; longer cooking will toughen the clams.

Remove chowder from heat and let stand a few minutes, then add hot milk, the clam liquor and seasoning to taste. By adding these last there is less chance of the chowder curdling, which often happens if seasonings are added before the hot milk.

Add 1 tablespoon butter just before serving, or place a bit in each soup bowl. Serves 6 or 8.

Clam Fritters

1 pint fresh clams
½ cup clam liquor
½ teaspoon salt
2 cups flour
2 teaspoons baking powder
2 eggs
1 cup milk

Sift flour, baking powder and salt. Add well beaten eggs, clam liquor and milk slowly to make batter, stir well. Grind clams (with coarse blades) in food chopper. Add to batter and drop on greased griddle or skillet. Cook about 8 minutes to a side. Serve hot. Serves 6.

Scallop Casserole

1 pound scallops, quartered
1 can mushroom soup (undiluted)
4 crushed saltines
2/3 green pepper, chopped
1 small can pimiento (or less)
¼ pound American cheese
½ teaspoon Worcestershire sauce
1 tablespoon lemon juice
3 tablespoons catsup

Pinch of baking soda

Parboil scallops using ½ cup of water. Mix all other ingredients together and put in baking dish. Cover with buttered crumbs. Bake at 350°F. for one-half hour or until done.

Escalloped Scallops

1 pound bay scallops
18 saltines (crushed)
1 pint milk
½ can undiluted mushroom soup
½ teaspoon accent
1 tablespoon butter

Soak scallops in milk 5 minutes then put in buttered casserole in layers with cracker crumbs. Make last layer crumbs. Top with soup and dot with butter.

Add remainder of milk to which accent has been added. Season with salt and pepper to taste. Bake 40 minutes at 350°.

Scallop Stew

1 pound scallops (remove hard ears)   1/3 cup butter
1 quart milk   ½ pint light cream

Heat in a heavy saucepan until milk skims over, add ½ teaspoon paprika, teaspoon salt and ½ teaspoon accent. Cool and reheat for better flavor. Stir well and serve with oyster crackers and pickles.

Baked Scallops

Wash fresh scallops in cold water, drain and dry well. Remove the hard piece from each one, which is on one side. Wipe carefully, roll in flour. Put in greased pan. Fill to about ½ the depth of scallops with rich milk. Dot with butter, salt and pepper to taste. When baked about ½ hour in medium oven (350°F.) turn each, and brown on other side.

These are very rich and good.

Do not cook in too hot an oven or the milk will curdle and be unsightly; and will also toughen the scallops. Serve at once.

Submitted by Miss Etta F. Beverage, North Haven, Maine

Broiled Scallops

Drain the scallops; if the large sea scallops are used, cut in halves crosswise. Dip in melted butter, roll in fine bread crumbs and place on a well oiled baking sheet or rack under the broiler. Brown on one side, turn and allow to brown delicately on the other. Serve garnished with sections of lemon and parsley and accompany with tartar sauce. A quart of scallops (2 pounds) will serve six people.

Seafood Newburg

2 cups cooked haddock (1 pound)
1 pound cooked scallops
5 pounds cooked lobster (1 pound meat)

Butter well a shallow casserole. Place seafood in casserole. Add 1½ teaspoons salt and cover with rich cream sauce and dot with butter. Bake in a 325° oven for 30 minutes. One-fourth cup of sherry may be mixed in just before serving.

RICH CREAM SAUCE

1 cup milk	3 tablespoons flour
½ cup cream	3 tablespoons butter

Prepare by adding flour to melted butter, then add to hot milk and cream. Stir until thick and salt and pepper to taste.

Manhattan Fish

Three pounds haddock or halibut, boiled, boned, flaked. Place in buttered casserole, cover with following sauce.

SAUCE

4 tablespoons oleo or butter	Pepper to taste
4 tablespoons flour	1½ cups tomato soup
2 cups milk	½ cup sharp cheese cut up
½ teaspoon salt	1 cup stuffed olives, sliced

Melt butter in saucepan. Add flour, blend and add milk and other ingredients. Cook until thickened. Pour over fish in casserole. Top with cracker crumbs. Bake 40 minutes in 350° oven.

Submitted by Mrs. Walter Ingerson, Vinalhaven, Maine

Manner of Frying Fish

After the fish is well cleaned lay on folded towel and dry out all the water. When well wiped and dry, roll in wheat flour to which has been added corn meal (2 tablespoons to ½ cup flour) and ½ teaspoon salt and a few grains of pepper.

Fry in a thick bottomed (iron) frying pan in ½ inch cooking oil very hot, lay fish in and fry gently until one side is delicate brown, then turn over. Take up carefully and serve quickly while hot.

Any fillets, smelts, trout, etc., can be done this way.

Stuffed Fish Fillets — Halibut

4 fish fillets	½ teaspoon salt
2 tablespoons chopped onion	¼ teaspoon thyme
¼ cup chopped celery	⅛ teaspoon pepper
2 tablespoons butter	1¼ cups soft bread crumbs
2 tablespoons milk, or more	
2 tablespoons chopped green pepper	
1½ cups cheese sauce (See Sauces)	

Wipe each fish fillet with a damp cloth. Saute the onion, celery, and green pepper in the butter for 6 to 8 minutes, or until tender but not brown. Add these vegetables to the bread crumbs with the salt, thyme, and pepper. Mix well. Add milk to moisten. Divide the stuffing in four equal parts. Put 1 portion on each fillet. Roll each fillet and fasten with a toothpick. Place rolled fillets in a shallow baking pan. Pour the cheese sauce over the fish. Bake in a moderate oven, 350 degrees for 30 minutes, or until the fish is tender. Serve at once.

Baked Haddock with Cheese

2 pounds haddock fillet	4 tablespoons butter
1 cup milk	¼ pound Amercian cheese
½ cup flour	1 tablespoon dry mustard

Make a sauce of flour, mustard, butter and milk (this will be very thick). When thick add cheese that has been cut up in small pieces. Continue to heat until cheese is melted.

Place layers of raw fish and cheese sauce in casserole and bake one hour at 350 degrees.

Boiled Haddock

Cook whole haddock in enough boiling water to cover, to which is added salt and lemon juice or vinegar. Lemon juice or vinegar keeps the flesh white.

Fish may be tied in a piece of cheesecloth to prevent it from breaking up or it will help to place it on a rack inside of kettle.

Boil fish gently until flesh leaves the bones, no matter how long the time.

Serve on a large platter with white sauce to which sliced hard cooked eggs have been added.

Boiled haddock with lobster sauce is a very special dinner.

Fish Casserole

Gently boil 5 or 6 pounds of haddock. Remove bones carefully and shred quite fine. Let 1 pint of milk, 1/4 of an onion and sprig of parsley come to a boil over low heat; then slowly stir in 1/2 cup flour, which has been stirred smooth with a cup of cold milk. Stir and cook sauce until it thickens. Add slightly beaten yolks of 2 eggs. Season with 1/2 teaspoon white pepper, 1/4 teaspoon thyme, 1/4 cup of butter and salt well. Butter a casserole and put in, first a layer of sauce, then one of fish. Finish with sauce and over it sprinkle cracker crumbs and a light grating of cheese. Bake one-half hour in moderate oven (350 degrees).

Submitted by Frank D. Rowe, Warren, Maine

Quoddy Fish Chowder

1/4 pound salt pork, cubed   1 teaspoon salt
4 cups of diced raw potatoes
3 pounds of fresh skinned haddock with bones in it
3 onions, sliced   1 tablespoon butter
2 cups whole milk, scalded   1/4 teaspoon pepper

Fry the salt pork out in the pot in which the chowder is to be made. Remove fried pork, put into the pot the onions, potatoes and half the salt. Cover with hot water and cook until potatoes are tender, but not broken. Cut the fish into three pieces, and in a separate dish simmer it in boiling water to which the remaining 1/2 teaspoon salt has been added. (This is to keep the fish from breaking up.) Then put fish and strained fish stock (for flavor) into heated chowder dish. Add milk, butter and pepper. Season to taste. Serves 5.

Baked Stuffed Whole Fish

Use whole fish, cleaned and dressed. Rub inside and outside of fish with salt, stuff loosely as stuffing will expand during cooking. Sew up opening in fish with needle and thread, or close with metal skewers. Place fish on greased rack in shallow, uncovered pan. Bake at 375°F., allowing 10 minutes per pound for fish under 4 pounds. Add 5 minutes per pound to cooking time for larger fish. If fish seems dry while cooking, baste occasionally with the juice from the bottom of the pan, or lay strips of bacon or salt pork across the fish.

STUFFING

2 cups soft fine bread crumbs
½ teaspoon mixed poultry seasoning
1 teaspoon salt
Pepper
1 tablespoon onion juice
2 tablespoons melted fat or butter
Milk enough to mix dressing (about ½ cup)

Baked Bass or Pike

STUFFING

1 quart bread cubes   ¾ teaspoon salt
3 tablespoons minced onion   ¼ teaspoon black pepper
1 teaspoon crushed sage leaves
¾ cup cooked celery (chopped fine)
6 tablespoons hot melted butter 4 tablespoons hot celery liquid

Cleanse and fill with stuffing. Sew up fish and cover with salt pork slices then, dredge with flour. Add 1 cup boiling water in shallow pan and lay fish in this and bake 1 hour; baste frequently. Remove the fish when done, add browned flour and butter to the gravy, cook a few minutes, then pour around fish on platter. Garnish with lemon and parsley.

Boiled Bass

½ cup vinegar
1 teaspoon salt
1 onion

1 dozen whole black peppers
1 blade of mace

Put in kettle of hot water enough for fish to swim in easily. Sew fish in a piece of clean net fitted to its shape. Heat slowly for first half hour, then boil eight minutes at least to the pound.

Unwrap and pour over it a cup of drawn butter, based upon the liquor in which the fish was boiled with the juice of half a lemon stirred in. Garnish with sliced lemon.

Flounders au Gratin

Parsley
Chives
1 cup mushrooms
2 pounds fillets of flounder
3 tablespoons butter

1 teaspoon salt
¼ teaspoon pepper
¾ cup bread crumbs
1 cup warm water

Butter an oval glass baking dish. Chop the parsley and chives. Peel the mushrooms and slice. Cover the bottom of the dish with half the mushrooms, parsley and chives. Arrange the fish on top and cover with remaining mushrooms, parsley and chives. Dot with 2 tablespoons of the butter and sprinkle with salt. Sprinkle with bread crumbs. Add 1 cup of warm water. Cook ½ hour and serve in the same dish.

Salmon Drop Cake

2 cups canned salmon, drained and flaked
1 small onion, chopped
½ cup cream
½ teaspoon salt

⅛ teaspoon pepper
½ teaspoon savory
3 eggs, separated

Prepare the salmon, carefully removing the bones. Add the onion, moisten with as much of the cream as is needed, season with the salt, pepper and savory. Stir in the yolks of the eggs, beat the whites stiff, and fold in. Drop the mixture by spoonfuls on a hot griddle, buttered; cook on one side, turn and cook on the other until a nice golden brown.

21

Soused Trout

Boil trout in small amount of salted water until cooked. Put them in dish, pour over half vinegar, half water and 1 tablespoon pickling spice which has been heated. Serve cold. This will keep fish 4 or 5 days. Mackerel or herring can be used instead of trout.

Pickled Mackerel

1 pound can mackerel (drained)
1 teaspoon whole mixed pickling spice   1 onion (sliced)
¾ cup vinegar   ¼ teaspoon pepper
¾ teaspoon salt

Place large pieces of mackerel in a shallow dish. Put vinegar, onion and other seasonings in a saucepan and bring to boil. Cool slightly, pour over fish and set in refrigerator to chill. Serve with crisp slices of cucumber if desired or pour off liquor and serve lettuce with mackerel on it.

NOTE — Fresh mackerel may be used in this recipe if whole fish is simmered until just tender in water seasoned with salt, pepper and bay leaf. Cool and proceed as with canned mackerel.

Submitted by Mrs. Harvard Bickford, Rockland, Maine

Baked Mackerel

2—1-1½ pound mackerel   1 cup milk
¼ cup flour   1 tablespoon parsley flakes
½ teaspoon salt   2 slices salt pork (thin)
⅛ teaspoon pepper

Wipe dry mackerel which have been split and washed. Put in shallow baking dish split side up, dredge with sifted flour, salt and pepper — lay pork slices on thick part. Sprinkle parsley over the entire fish. Add milk to pan and bake in 400° oven a half hour. Serves 4. Garnish with lemon and fresh parsley.

Soused Clams

Remove steamed clams from shells and use for soused clams.

For one quart of these clams use 1½ cups of clam liquor to ½ cup of vinegar and season with pepper. Sufficient amount of clam liquor-vinegar mixture should be used to cover dish of clams. Cover and store in refrigerator overnight. These are good warm or cold.

Tuna Salad

2 cans (6½ or 7 ounces each) tuna
1 clove garlic, peeled and quartered
½ cup salad or olive oil
1 cup ½ inch bread cubes
8 cups mixed salad greens
¼ teaspoon salt
Dash freshly ground black pepper
1 egg, cooked 1 minute
1 tablespoon lemon juice
¼ cup grated Parmesan cheese

Drain tuna; flake. Add garlic to oil and let stand at least 1 hour. Place bread cubes in a shallow baking pan and toast in a moderate oven, 350°F., stirring occasionally until bread is lightly browned on all sides. Remove garlic from oil. Gradually pour ¼ cup of garlic oil over toasted bread cubes, mixing lightly until all the oil is absorbed. Place salad greens, torn into bite-size pieces, in a large salad bowl. Sprinkle with salt and pepper. Pour remaining garlic oil over greens, tossing lightly. Break egg into salad. Add lemon juice and mix thoroughly. Add grated cheese, bread cubes, and tuna; toss lightly. Serve immediately. Serves 6.

Chinese Tuna

1 cup chopped celery
1 cup chopped onion
½ green pepper chopped
1 can chow mein noodles
1 can tuna
1 can cream of mushroom soup
¾ cup water

Combine celery, onion and pepper in a frypan with one-third cup of water and one tablespoon of butter. Saute until tender.

Reserve one-third of the can of noodles for the topping; and add the rest to tuna, soup, water, sauted onions, pepper and celery. Add salt and pepper to taste. Pour into casserole, top with noodles and bake at 350°F. for 30 minutes.

Submitted by Mrs. Christine McMahon, Rockland, Maine

23

Fishman's Stuffed Tomato

4 ounce can tuna fish
½ cup diced celery
¼ cup shredded cheddar cheese
¾ teaspoon salt
⅛ teaspoon ground black pepper

¼ teaspoon garlic powder
2 tablespoons mayonnaise
¾ teaspoon chopped onion
6 medium fresh tomatoes
Chicory

Drain oil from tuna fish and flake. Combine with next seven ingredients. Remove stem ends of tomatoes and cut into three cross-wise slices. Put together in layer cake fashion using the tuna fish mixture as filling. Arrange on a bed of chicory. Serves 6.

Submitted by Mrs. Maude Barstow, Rockland, Maine

Maine Sardine Casserole

2 cans (4 ounces each) Maine sardines
2 tablespoons chopped onion
2 tablespoons melted fat or oil
2 tablespoons flour
1½ teaspoons salt
Dash pepper
2 teaspoons Worcestershire sauce
1½ quarts sliced cooked potatoes

2 cups milk
1 cup grated cheese

Drain sardines. Reserve 6 sardines for top. Cook onion in fat until tender. Blend in flour and seasonings. Add milk gradually and cook until thick, stirring constantly. Add cheese and Worcestershire sauce; stir until cheese melts. Arrange half of the potatoes, the sardines, and the remaining potatoes in layers in a well-greased 2-quart casserole. Cover with the cheese sauce. Garnish with the 6 sardines. Bake in a moderate oven, 350°F., for 25 to 30 minutes or until heated. Serves 6.

Fairy Umbrellas

12 mushrooms
½ teaspoon salt

1 tablespoon lemon juice
French dressing

FILLING

3 hard cooked eggs, riced

¼ cup sardines, mashed

½ teaspoon condiment sauce

½ teaspoon scraped onion

Salt

Mayonnaise

Wash the mushrooms, remove the stems and peel them. Place the caps and stems in a saucepan with warm water to cover, add the salt and lemon juice and simmer 10 minutes. Drain and cool. Marinate with French dressing and chill for 2 hours. Drain and stuff the caps with the filling. Insert the stems as the handles of the umbrellas. Serve as appetizers.

Fillling: Blend the eggs, sardines, condiment sauce and onion. Season with salt and moisten with mayonnaise.

Codfish Rarebit

1 cup salt codfish, freshened (or leftover boiled fish)

1 tablespoon butter

1 tablespoon flour

¼ teaspoon onion juice

1 teaspoon pimento, minced

1 cup rich milk

1 egg, beaten

¾ cup grated cheese, optional

Break codfish in small pieces. Melt butter, add flour, onion juice and pimento. Mix thoroughly. Add milk gradually, then fish and cheese. Cook until all is blended, add egg and cook 5 minutes longer. Serve at once on toast.

New England Salt Codfish with Pork Scraps

Break salt codfish into pieces and cover with cold water and bring slowly to simmering point, but do not boil. Drain and repeat two more times using cold water and bringing to simmering point until salt fish is fresh enough to suit you. If fish boils it will be tough. Serve with potatoes boiled with the skins on and fry out salt pork, using hot fat and pork scraps over salt fish and potatoes.

Pickled beets or onion slices in vinegar add to this old-time dinner.

Pork Scraps — Cut up ¼ pound fat salt pork in very small cubes. Place in small black frying pan and simmer slowly until salt pork becomes crispy.

Yankee Codfish in Gravy

Cook the salt codfish as in the preceding recipe. Drain. Make a rich white sauce as follows: Melt 2 tablespoons butter in a double boiler, add 2 tablespoons flour and blend well. Add 1 cup milk and cook until thickened stirring constantly. Stir in a slightly beaten egg and season.

Place fish on a large platter and pour the gravy over it. Serve piping hot with hot baked potatoes.

Pickled beets or buttered beets also add to this Yankee Dinner. Some Down - Easterners prefer adding sliced hard cooked eggs to the white sauce in place of the slightly beaten egg.

Penobscot Alewives

1 alewife per person

Prepare by cutting off fins and head. Clean out insides and peel off skin. Put fish in frying pan (iron is best). Cover with cold water. Cover tightly and put on high heat. When water boils, fish is done.

Warren Alewives

1 alewife per person

Prepare by wrapping entire fish as is, in freezer foil and putting in a hot oven (400°). Bake for 30 minutes. Serve in foil.

Landlubber Special

2 pounds yellow perch fillets or other fish fillets, fresh or frozen
1 teaspoon salt   ¼ cup melted fat or oil
Dash pepper   3 slices bacon (optional)
Bread stuffing

Thaw frozen fillets. Skin fillets and sprinkle both sides with salt and pepper. Line 12 well-greased muffin tins with fillets, overlapping ends of fillets. Fill the center of each with bread stuffing. Brush tops with melted fat and place ¼ slice of bacon on each. Bake in a moderate oven (350°F.) for 25 to 30 minutes or until fish flakes easily when tested with a fork. Serves 6.

BREAD STUFFING

¾ cup chopped celery

¼ cup chopped onion   1 quart day-old bread crumbs

1/3 cup melted fat or oil   1 teaspoon salt

1 teaspoon thyme, sage, or savory seasoning   Dash pepper

Cook celery and onion in fat until tender. Combine all ingredients; mix thoroughly. If stuffing seems very dry, add 1 tablespoon water, milk, or fish stock to moisten.

Broiled Trout

6 pan-dressed trout or other small fish, fresh or frozen

1 cup melted fat or oil   2 cloves garlic, finely chopped

¼ cup chopped parsley   2 teaspoons basil

2 tablespoons catsup   1 teaspoon salt

2 tablespoons wine vinegar   ¼ teaspoon pepper

Thaw frozen fish. Clean, wash, and dry fish. Place in a single layer in a shallow baking dish. Combine remaining ingredients. Pour sauce over fish and let stand for 30 minutes, turning once. Remove fish, reserving sauce for basting. Place fish on a well-greased broiler pan. Brush with sauce. Broil about 3 inches from source of heat, 5 to 7 minutes or until lightly browned, basting twice. Turn carefully and brush other side with sauce. Broil 5 to 7 minutes longer, basting occasionally, until fish is brown and flakes easily when tested with a fork. Serves 6.

Finnan Haddie in Milk

Cover the fish with water and simmer for a few minutes. Drain and add 1 cup warm milk and 2 tablespoons butter. Place in the oven to keep warm, but do not leave long enough for the milk to curdle. (The fish is simmered in water because the smoke in the fish would curdle the milk, if it were cooked in milk first.) Serve with a garnish of parsley. 2 pound fish will serve 6. Serve with buttermilk biscuits.

Corned Hake

Buy a whole hake and have the fish dealer corn (salt) it for you. Let the salt stay on the fish overnight.

The fresh hake can be cooked in well salted water if not corned overnight, but is not quite so tasty.

Place corned hake in a fish bag made of cheesecloth or place on a rack in the bottom of a kettle. Cover fish with water and boil gently until fish is tender.

Serve fish with hot boiled potatoes, boiled beets and a fish sauce with sliced hard boiled eggs.

For two cups of fish or white sauce add ¼ cup of flour to ¼ cup melted butter. Mix in two cups of hot milk and cook in the top of the double boiler until thick. Season with salt and pepper. Then add two sliced hard cooked eggs to the sauce. Serve hot with the corned hake.

Fish Cakes

Two pounds salt fish soaked overnight in cold water or parboiled 30 minutes, chopped fine with 12 mashed potatoes, 2 well beaten eggs, ¼ cup milk, dash of pepper. Make into cakes and roll in flour. Fry in hot fat a few minutes on each side.

Veal in Cream

2 pounds veal cut in small cubes
2 tablespoons flour 1 cup sour or sweet cream
½ teaspoon salt   ¾ cup or 14 ounce can sliced mushrooms
2 tablespoons butter 1 tablespoon onion juice

Brown veal and place in casserole. Add 3 tablespoons water and stir to make brown gravy for sauce, add flour to make smooth paste. Add seasonings and cream, when thickened remove from heat, add mushrooms and onion juice. Pour over veal and bake ¾ hour at 300 degrees. Serves 4.

Corn Meal Mush or Hasty Pudding

(1887 Cook Book)

Put two quarts of water into a clean dinner pot or stewpan, cover it and let it become boiling hot over the fire; then add a tablespoonful of salt, take off the light scum from the top, have sweet, fresh yellow or white corn meal; take a handful of the meal with the left hand and a pudding stick in the right, then with the stick, stir the water around and by degrees let fall the meal; when one handful is exhausted, refill it; continue to stir and add meal until it is as thick as you can stir easily, or until the stick will stand in it; stir it awhile longer; let the fire be gentle; when it is sufficiently cooked, which will be in half an hour, it will bubble or puff up; turn it into a deep basin. This is good eaten cold or hot, with milk or with butter and syrup or sugar, or with meat and gravy, the same as potatoes or rice.

Many "Down Easterners" remember Sunday night suppers consisting of hot Corn Meal Mush and milk served with stripped salt codfish on the side.

FRIED MUSH

Turn the above recipe of hot mush into bread tins and when cold slice it, dip each piece in flour and fry it in lard or butter mixed in the frying pan, turning to brown well on both sides. Must be served hot. A good breakfast or supper dish with syrup.

Maine Baked Beans

2 pounds dry beans	1 teaspoon dry mustard
½ pound salt pork	½ teaspoon pepper
½ cup sugar	1½ teaspoons salt
¼ cup molasses	

Pick over beans and soak overnight in cold water. In morning parboil until skins crack when blown upon. Put in bean pot and add salt pork (cut down to rind to make cubes) on top. Mix sugar, molasses, mustard, pepper and salt with 1 pint of boiling water, pour over beans and pork. Bake at 300 degrees 6 hours. Add water when necessary.

New England Boiled Dinner

4 pounds corned beef brisket	6 medium parsnips
6 medium potatoes	6 onions (optional)
1 yellow turnip	1 small cabbage
6 medium carrots	6 medium beets

Cover meat with cold water, bring to a boil, then lower the heat and allow the meat to simmer gently for 3 hours or until tender. In the meantime cook beets separately to serve with the corned beef. About 1 hour before the meat is done skim it free of excess fat, add turnips, carrots, potatoes and quartered cabbage. Continue cooking and add parsnips during the last twenty minutes of cooking. Continue cooking until all is tender. Onions may be added to the vegetables, if you desire.

Serve sliced meat on platter, with vegetables. Pass chili sauce, mustard, mustard pickles, horseradish, or vinegar.

Red Flannel Hash

2 cups cold cooked meat	2½ cups potatoes (cooked)
¾ cup turnip (cooked)	¼ teaspoon pepper
¾ cup parsnips (cooked)	½ teaspoon salt
¾ cup carrots (cooked)	¼ cup water
1 cup cabbage (cooked)	4 teaspoons garlic vinegar
1 cup beets (cooked)	
½ cup raw onions warmed in 2 tablespoons butter	

Dice vegetables and combine all ingredients in a black iron frying pan — lastly pour over the ¼ cup of water. Cover and let cook slowly. Stir occasionally until thoroughly heated and the flavors are blended.

Potato Croquettes

Take 2 cups of cold mashed potato, season with a pinch of salt, pepper, and a tablespoonful of butter. Beat up the whites of 2 eggs, and work all together thoroughly; make it into small balls slightly flattened, dip them in the beaten yolks of the eggs, then roll either in flour or cracker crumbs; fry the same as fish balls.

Vegetarian Loaf

Boil and mash 8 medium sized potatoes. Put through the food chopper the following: 3 medium sized onions, 2 slices white bread, 2 shredded wheat, and ½ cup nut meats. Add 1½ level teaspoons sage and 1 teaspoon salt, butter size of an egg, 1 egg well beaten, and 1/3 cup sweet milk. Mix thoroughly and bake in a loaf about 1 hour. Pour a little milk over top before putting in oven, about 2 tablespoons. Bake in 375° oven.

Submitted by Mabel Holbrook, Camden, Maine

Chicken Roly-Poly

(1887 Cook Book)

One quart of flour, two teaspoonfuls of cream of tartar mixed with the flour, one teaspoonful of soda dissolved in a teacupful of milk; a teaspoonful of salt; do not use shortening of any kind, but roll out the mixture half an inch thick, and on it lay minced chicken, veal or mutton. The meat must be seasoned with pepper and salt and be free from gristle. Roll the crust over and over, and put it on a buttered plate and place in a steamer for half an hour. Serve for breakfast or lunch, giving a slice to each person with gravy served with it.

Hot Dog Deluxe

1 pound frankfurts	Small onion
Stale bread	4 strips bacon
Poultry seasoning	

Make dressing according to individual taste from bread, onion, poultry seasoning and salt.

Put a layer of dressing in greased casserole, add a layer of sliced frankfurts(cooked or raw) then a layer of dressing, and so on. Lay strips of bacon on top and bake in medium oven 20 to 30 minutes (as to frankfurts). Raw potatoes may be used the same way, but needs longer to cook. Hamburg may also be used.

Submitted by Miss Etta F. Beverage, North Haven, Maine

Pork Chops Deluxe

Spread a thin coat of prepared mustard over 6 pork chops cut ¾ inch thick. In a paper bag put ¼ cup flour, 1 teaspoon salt and ¼ teaspoon pepper. Shake chops in this mixture.

Brown chops in 2 tablespoons melted fat. Place chops in baking dish and pour 1 can chicken rice soup over them. Cover and bake at 350° for about 40 minutes. Serves 6.

Submitted by Miss Etta F. Beverage, North Haven, Maine

Chicken Curry

(Miss Parlan's Cook Book 1880)

1 chicken weighing 3 pounds
¾ cup butter
2 large onions
1 heaping tablespoon curry powder
3 tomatoes or 1 cup of the canned article
Enough cayenne to cover a silver three-cent piece
Salt   1 cup milk

Put the butter and onions, cut fine, on to cook. Stir all the while until brown; then put in the chicken which has been cut in small pieces, the curry, the tomatoes, salt and pepper. Stir well· Cover tightly and let simmer one hour, stirring occasionally; then add milk. Boil up once, and serve with boiled rice. This makes a very rich and hot curry but for the real lover of the dish, none too much so.

Chicken Pie

Cook 6 pound fowl in salted water (1½ teaspoons salt and 1½ quarts water) until meat comes off bones. Take out of broth and cool. Pick meat off bones in large pieces. Lay in casserole. Bring the broth to a boil and add ½ cup cut up celery, 1 large carrot, cut up, and 1 large onion. Cook until vegetables are done. Thicken for gravy, using ¼ cup flour. Pour over meat in casserole while boiling and put ½ can of undiluted mushroom soup on top. Then top with cut out biscuits.

BISCUITS

2 cups flour
7 tablespoons of chicken fat or shortening
1 teaspoon salt
3 teaspoons baking powder   1 cup milk

Cook in 450° oven 10 minutes then reduce to 375° for 30 minutes.

Creamy Chicken Fricassee

1 stewing chicken, cut up   1/3 cup finely chopped onions
1/3 cup finely chopped celery   2 cups milk
A few celery leaves   10 tablespoons flour
2 bay leaves   Salt and pepper
4 or 5 cups boiling water

Put chicken, celery, onion, celery leaves and bay leaves in a large heavy kettle. Add water. Cover and simmer over low heat for 2 hours, or until chicken is tender.

When chicken is tender, remove from stock to a hot platter. Also remove and discard celery leaves and bay leaves. Skim off excess fat from top of stock. Boil down stock to about 2 cups.

Add milk gradually to flour, stirring until smooth. Add milk-flour mixture to hot stock, mix well. Cook, stirring constantly, until thick. Season to taste with salt and pepper. Pour gravy over chicken or serve separately. Serve with hot fluffy rice, dumplings or biscuits. Serves 4 to 6.

DUMPLINGS

2 cups flour   2 tablespoons fat
4 teaspoons baking powder   1 cup milk
1 teaspoon salt

Sift dry ingredients, cut in fat, add milk. Drop by spoonfuls on top of stew. Cover tightly. Cook for 12 minutes. Do not open until 12 minutes up.

33

Cucumbers

A troublesome but sure way is to cover them with hot brine (not too strong), scalding and pouring it over them for eight successive days. Then wipe the cucumbers very carefully, and put them in a good spiced vinegar. Your work is done for a century if need be.

Rockland Congregational Society Cook Book — 1886

Barbecued Chicken with Maine Barbecue Sauce

2—2½ pound State of Maine broilers, split in half

1 cup vinegar   ½ cup cooking oil
1 cup water   1 tablespoon salt

Mix vinegar, water, oil and salt. Stir frequently. If butter is used in place of oil — 1 pint cooking oil equals 1 pound butter. Place broiler halves on a rack 15 to 18 inches from lighted charcoal. Turn the chicken and baste frequently to prevent burning. Plan on an hour's cooking time. When the leg bone turns easily when twisted the chicken is done. Remember — slow cooking is the secret of delicious barbecued chicken.

English Yorkshire Pudding

1 cup of flour – scant   2 eggs
1/3 teaspoon salt   1 cup of milk

Mix flour and salt. Beat eggs thoroughly and add milk and stir into first mixture. Beat vigorously with egg beater for two minutes. Pour into hot oiled muffin tins (about ½ teaspoon fat in each tin). If desired one can use a pan 10 x 13 oiled and heated (about 2 tablespoons bacon fat). Bake 25 minutes in 400° oven.

HAVE ALL COOKED

1 pound stew beef   Salt and peper to taste
1 large onion cut in pieces

Cover with water and stew until meat is tender. Add more water as needed. Thicken gravy slightly by mixing 1½ tablespoons flour and ¼ cup of water; add to gravy until thickness desired. This meat and gravy are poured over each serving of Yorkshire Pudding and should be served at once. This is a very delicious dish served with any vegetable.

Submitted by Mrs. Ingrid Nelson, Rockland, Maine

Mulligan Stew

(Very Old, Handed Down For Generations)

Onion, carrot, celery, and turnip, ½ cup each diced; 4 potatoes cut in quarters. Add to ⅛ pound salt pork — 2 pounds *venison cut in small pieces and cooked 1 hour in 1 pint of water, 1 teaspoon salt, and a few grains of pepper. Cook all together 1 hour.

DUMPLINGS are added the last 12 minutes — 1 cup flour, 2 teaspoons baking powder, ½ teaspoon sugar, ½ teaspoon salt, and ½ cup milk. Stir together and drop by spoonful on boiling stew.

*Lamb or beef can be used.

Brunswick Stew

2½ pounds chicken, cut up	1 cup diced potato
1 pound plate beef, cut up	2 cups tomatoes
1 cup cooked lima beans	3 sliced onions
1 cup corn	Salt and pepper

Place chicken and beef in a heavy aluminum or iron kettle, cover with water and simmer until the meat is tender. Add the vegetables and seasonings. Simmer two more hours to blend the meats and vegetables thoroughly and to thicken the stew. Serve with corn bread.

Irish Stew

(Lamb and Rice)

3 pounds neck of lamb	Salt and pepper
5 onions	2 quarts of water
½ cup rice	

Cut meat in small pieces. Cover with boiling water, add sliced onions and rice. Simmer three hours. About one-half hour before serving season with salt and pepper. Dumplings may be added at this time also.

35

Barbecued Spareribs

3 to 4 pounds ribs cut in pieces 1 large onion
1 lemon   1/3 cup Worcestershire sauce
1 cup catsup   1 teaspoon salt
1 teaspoon chili powder   2 cups water
2 dashes Tabasco

Place ribs in shallow pan meaty side up — on each add a slice of unpeeled lemon and a slice of onion. Roast at 450 degrees 30 minutes. Combine other ingredients and bring to boiling point and pour over ribs — reduce heat to 350 degrees. Baste every 15 minutes. Serves 4.

Irish Stew

(Beef and Vegetable)

2 pounds top of the round of beef
1 large onion, sliced   4 potatoes, pared and sliced
2 teaspoons salt   3 slices yellow turnip
⅛ teaspoon pepper   4 tablespoons flour
2 carrots, diced

Wipe the beef and cut into small pieces. Reserve the edge trimmings to try out. Roll the pieces of beef in flour and sear in the fat. Place the meat in a kettle with the onion, salt and pepper. Cover with about 2 quarts of cold water and simmer until the meat is tender. Add the carrots, the potatoes and turnip. Moisten the flour with cold water to form a paste. Add to stew and allow to simmer until slightly thickened. At this point, care is required that the stew does not burn. Bring to the boiling point and serve. The flour paste may be omitted if you prefer. Good with dumplings.

Old-Time Scalloped Potatoes

6 cups thinly sliced pared potatoes   2 cups hot milk
2 cups thinly sliced onions   Salt and pepper
5 tablespoons flour   Paprika
4 tablespoons butter

Start heating oven to 400°F. Arrange layer of potatoes in buttered casserole. Cover with a layer of onions. Sprinkle with some of the flour, salt and pepper; dot with some of the butter. **Repeat** layers until all are used, ending with butter. Pour hot milk over **all**; sprinkle with paprika, if you wish. Bake uncovered for at least **one** hour, lowering the temperature of the oven to 350 degrees or **lower** after the milk begins to bubble. Cook until tender.

Leg of Lamb

With Pineapple Stuffing

Leg of lamb, bone removed	½ teaspoon salt
2 tablespoons minced onion	⅛ teaspoon pepper
2 tablespoons melted butter	1 tablespoon minced parsley
2 cups bread crumbs	1 cup crushed pineapple

Select a well meated leg of lamb and have the bone removed for stuffing. Cook minced onion in melted butter until tender; add the bread crumbs, salt, pepper, parsley and the crushed pineapple well drained.

Stuff the cavity with the mixture and secure the opening with skewers. Rub the outside of the leg with salt and pepper. Place on a rack in an open roasting pan, bake for the first 15 minutes at 500 degrees, then pour over the lamb the juice drained from the pineapple. Reduce heat to 350 degrees and finish baking.

Hot Pot of Beef and Barley

(Old-time Recipe)

Cut up in inch cubes one and one-half pounds of any red meat — yearling mutton, chuck beef or fresh pork — and brown in a hot, greaseless pan. Place in a stewpan with two quarts of water, three-fourths a cup of pearl barley, two teaspoons of salt, one tablespoon of vinegar, two carrots sliced, two large onions, chopped or grated, a small bunch of kitchen bouquet or soup greens, and simmer for an hour and a half. Then add six potatoes, pared and cut in halves, and cook until these are soft. Six large portions at five cents a portion.

Scotch Steak and Kidney Pie

3 pounds top round steak	Flour
2 veal kidneys	Butter
Onions	Salt and pepper
Worcestershire sauce	Baking powder

Trim all fat, veins and gristle from steak and melt fat in frying pan, discard solid, keep liquid. Cut meat in squares (1½ x 1½). Sift into large bowl 1 cup flour; wet meat and press into flour, getting as much flour as possible into each piece of meat. Heat large pot and ⅛ inch of fat on medium heat — when sizzling hot add floured steak, brown on both sides, add 1 tablespoon salt, ¼ teaspoon pepper, and ¾ tablespoon Worcestershire sauce. Add 3 small onions, chopped finely. Prepare kidney: Cut off all meat, clear off any fat or root. Cut in small pieces and boil in two waters three minutes — throw out each water — add kidneys to pot of meat. Cover, allow to simmer 2 hours. Be sure to stir during last hour of cooking to prevent sticking. After 2 hours, remove meat to casserole and strain gravy over it. Now chill until ready for crust.

CRUST: 1 cup flour, 2 teaspoons baking powder and ½ teaspoon salt, sift together, add 1/3 cup shortening. Mix well and add water enough to roll out. Fit over meat in casserole. Make holes for steam. Bake at 375 degrees until golden.

Hearty Vegetable Soup

1 pound beef chuck plus 1 knuckle

5½ cups water	½ cup potatoes (raw, diced)
1 teaspoon salt	¾ cup carrots (diced)
Few grains of pepper	2—1 pound cans tomatoes
¾ cup onion (minced)	1 tablespoon sugar
2/3 cup celery (diced)	2 tablespoons rice (raw)

Add water and seasonings to beef and bones, which has been fat trimmed and cut into small pieces, simmer until meat is tender about 1½ hours, add rice and cook ½ hour, then add vegetables and sugar and cook until vegetables are done. (129 calories to a serving.)

Ragout of Lamb or Mutton

2 pounds lamb or mutton
1 tablespoon butter
1 tablespoon flour
1 diced onion
1 diced carrot

2 cups hot water
1 teaspoon salt
$\frac{1}{4}$ teaspoon pepper
1 bay leaf
1 cup peas, fresh or canned

Wipe meat with damp cloth, cut in 1 inch pieces. Melt butter in saucepan, stir in flour. Add meat, carrot, and onion. Cook 20 minutes, stirring often. Add hot water, salt, pepper and bay leaf, bring to boil. Cover tightly, let simmer 2 hours. Remove bay leaf, add peas. Simmer 20 minutes more. Serve hot. Serves 6.

MINT SAUCE

Chop enough leaves and tender tops of mint to fill 1 cup. Add $\frac{1}{4}$ cup sugar and $\frac{1}{2}$ cup vinegar. Prepare an hour before using, allowing the mint flavor to be absorbed.

Oven Baked French Fried Potatoes

8 to 10 medium potatoes
1/3 cup salad oil or melted vegetable shortening
Salt and pepper

Preheat oven to 450°F. Wash, pare and cut potatoes in lengthwise strips, one-quarter to one-half inch thick, soaking in cold water 15 minutes. Dry between folds of a clean towel.

Pour one-half of the fat in a baking pan, place potatoes in pan and pour the remaining fat over them, turning potatoes over until all potatoes are coated with fat. Salt and pepper the potatoes and cook in a hot oven, turning occasionally, until they are golden brown, about 30 to 40 minutes. These are especially good with steak.

Ham with Sweet Potatoes

4 slices canned pineapple
2 large raw sweet potatoes, peeled
2 tart apples

1 slice raw ham
2/3 cup pineapple juice
Whole cloves
$\frac{1}{2}$ cup brown sugar

In the bottom of an eight-inch greased casserole place the pineapple slices, cut the rings to fit the dish. On top of the pineapple place the sweet potatoes which have been peeled and cut in strips. Over the sweet potatoes place the apples which have been sliced thin, and on top of all place a slice of raw ham. Pour the pineapple juice over all. Stick whole cloves into the ham and sprinkle with brown sugar. Cover and bake about 2 hours at 325°F.

Navy Bean Soup

½ cup dried navy beans
1 ham bone
1 carrot, diced
1 onion, diced

1 potato, diced
4 cups boiling water
Salt and pepper

Pick over the beans, wash; cover with cold water and soak overnight. In the morning add the remaining ingredients and cook slowly until the beans are tender. This will require 2 to 3 hours. Remove the ham bone. Press vegetables through a sieve and thin to the desired consistency with hot water if necessary. Season to taste. Garnish with minced parsley.

Parsnip Stew

Peel and cut into bits a quart each of parsnips and potatoes. Fry out one slice of salt pork or 2 tablespoons of butter and put into a kettle and add potatoes and parsnips alternately, add ½ teaspoon salt, few grains of pepper, and 1½ cups water. Cover and cook steadily for ½ hour. Then stir and add more butter and a pint of milk. Set aside a short time before serving. Some like this better without the addition of milk.

Johnny Cake
(Over 100 Years Old)

½ cup corn meal
1 teaspoon salt   1 cup scalded milk or boiling water
Add salt to corn meal. Gradually stir in milk or water. Spread ¼ inch deep in buttered shallow pan. Dot with bits of butter. Bake at 350° until crisp. Split and spread with butter.

Pea Soup

1 pound dry peas (½ whole – ½ split)
2 quarts boiling water   1 onion (coarsely chopped)
1 smoked ham shank or bone   Salt and pepper to taste

Rinse ham shank or bone, add with chopped onion to boiling water. Rinse dry peas in cold water, drain and add with ham bone or shank. Boil moderately for two and one-half hours. Stir occasionally to prevent scorching. Remove shank at end of first hour and pick off pieces of ham to be served as garnish for soup. Serves 8 persons. Serve with Johnny Cake or Corn Bread.

Camp Coffee

½ cup coffee   6 cups freshly boiling water
1 egg   Few grains of salt
1 cup cold water

Wash egg, break and beat slightly, dilute with half the cold water, crush shell and add, mix with coffee. Add salt. Turn all into coffee pot (some use a cheese cloth bag — it's not necessary). Pour on freshly boiling water and stir. Stuff spout or cover tightly to keep in aroma. Set over direct heat and bring to boil, simmer 3 minutes. Add rest of cold water to settle. Set aside on warm stove until served— it is ready at once.

Prontos

2 cups biscuit mix   1 teaspoon vanilla
¼ cup sugar   Cinnamon and nutmeg
1/3 cup evaporated milk or light cream
1 egg
1/3 cup sugar

In medium bowl stir together biscuit mix, ¼ cup sugar, milk, vanilla, egg, ¼ teaspoon cinnamon and ½ teaspoon nutmeg until well blended. Place dough on well-floured surface and knead 10 times; roll to ⅜ inch thick and cut with doughnut cutter or cut in strips to make bow knots. Fry as doughnuts in 1 inch hot oil or fat and roll while warm in 1/3 cup sugar and ¼ teaspoon cinnamon and ½ teaspoon nutmeg. Makes 12. Serve warm.

Foil Baked Potatoes

Baking sized potato (1 per person)
Drippings from meat or bacon fat
Wash and dry potatoes, rub lightly with drippings. Place each potato on square of aluminum foil and wrap tightly. Bake at 425 degrees 1 hour and 10 minutes.

Campers Skillagalee

Bacon fat
1 raw Maine Potato for each camper
Salt and pepper

Heat bacon fat to cover bottom of an iron spider or fry pan. Pare and thinly slice raw potato, add to hot fat. With a spatula keep turning to prevent burning. Allow to cook and brown, then add salt and pepper to season.

Stovies

4 large Maine Potatoes   ½ teaspoon salt
2 medium onions   ⅛ teaspoon pepper
¼ cup butter or pork fat

Pare and cut potatoes and onions in ⅛ inch slices. Melt butter in heavy frying pan or (4 slices of salt pork may be tried out and fat used, as well as crispy meat). Add potatoes, onions, salt, pepper and water to cover partially. Use tight lid, cover closely. Cook until vegetables are tender and water absorbed. Serves 6.

No Bake Cookies

1 stick of oleo   3 tablespoons cocoa
2 cups sugar   ½ cup evaporated milk

Bring to boil — remove in one minute. Add ½ cup crunchy peanut butter, 3 cups quick oats, and 1 teaspoon vanilla. Stir in well until it loses its shine. Drop by teaspoons on waxed paper, let set 10 minutes.

Fried Apples

Beat 2 eggs, 1 tablespoon sugar, and 3 tablespoons sifted flour. Slice 4 tart apples, dip in batter and fry in butter or oil, take up on paper towel and sprinkle with sugar. Serve hot.

Corned Beef Hash

2 cups chopped cooked or canned corned beef
2 cups chopped, cooked potatoes   1 tablespoon minced onion
2 tablespoons fat   Pepper

Chop meat and potatoes separately, having them fine but not mashed. Heat a frying pan, melt fat and panfry the onion in it for about 3 minutes. Then add the beef, potatoes and pepper. When heated thoroughly allow hash to brown, then fold over like an omelet and transfer to a hot platter. If hash seems too dry, add 1 or 2 tablespoons hot milk or water. Serves 6. Any other chopped, cooked meat may be substituted for corned beef.

Fried Scone

To the recipe for buttermilk biscuits add 2 tablespoons sugar for each 2 cups of flour used and ½ cup of currants. Rinse currants off with boiling water to soften; drain, add to the dry ingredients. Follow directions for mixing and rolling biscuit dough and cut in pie shape wedges. Grease lightly black frying pan and fry dough over medium hot heat until both sides are golden brown. Turn down heat and finish cooking slowly until centers are cooked. Do not use too much fat in fry pan. These may be baked, but the old fashioned way is to cook them on top of the stove.

Note: This is a good recipe for campers as biscuit mix may be used with or without currants; add 2 tablespoons of sugar to each 2 cups of mix and follow other directions, and fry as above.

Potato Stew

Pare and slice one quart of potatoes; put on two slices fat salt pork; fry nice and brown, add one onion chopped fine, and one tablespoon flour; stir well to prevent burning. Add one quart boiling water and potatoes; boil until soft then add one cup rich milk and one-half dozen "old fashioned" crackers. One large spoonful butter may be added.

Rabbit Stew

1 rabbit (3 to 4 pounds)
1 cup wine vinegar
1 cup sliced onion
2 teaspoons salt
½ teaspoon cloves
¼ teaspoon thyme

¾ teaspoon red pepper sauce
1 cup flour
1 teaspoon salt
½ cup shortening
1 cup water
2 teaspoons sugar

Cut rabbit into serving pieces. Combine vinegar, onion, salt and seasonings. Marinate 5 hours. Strain reserve marinade. Combine flour and salt, coat the pieces of rabbit. Heat shortening in large skillet and add rabbit until brown. Drain fat. Add marinade. Cover and simmer 45 minutes. Stir. Add sugar. Serves 4.

Haunch of Venison Roasted

12 pounds roast
4 cups flour
2 cups water

Salt, pepper and flour dredge
1 tablespoon currant jelly

Wipe meat carefully with wet cloth and cover with a large sheet of buttered paper. Make a thick paste of flour and water, roll out ¾ inch thick and lay over the fat side of the haunch. Cover with three or four sheets of white paper and tie securely with cord. Put in dripping pan and roast, basting frequently to prevent paper and string from burning. A twelve pound haunch will take 3 hours to roast. Half an hour before it is done, remove from the oven, cut strings, take off paste and paper; dredge with flour, salt and pepper; return to the oven and roast to a fine brown. Serve with a brown sauce to which a tablespoon of currant jelly has been added.

Muster Gingerbread (Civil War)

1 cup molasses
1 cup sugar (scant)
½ cup melted shortening

½ cup sour milk (buttermilk)
1 teaspoon cinnamon
Ginger and salt

2 teaspoons soda dissolved in a little warm water. Flour to roll out. Add seedless raisins. Bake at 375 degrees for nearly 20 minutes.

1776 Molasses Dumplings

2 cups flour	2 teaspoons fat
1 teaspoon salt	2 teaspoons cream tartar
1 teaspoon soda	3/4 cup milk

Mix dumplings and roll to one inch thickness. Cut with small cutter. Drop 2 or 3 at a time in hot fat. Have ready another kettle of boiling molasses, as soon as fried drop into boiling molasses – remove and drain.

Apple Fritters (1850)

Make a batter in the proportion of one cup sweet milk to two cups flour, a heaping teaspoonful of baking powder, two eggs beaten separately, one tablespoon of sugar, and a teaspoonful of salt; heat the milk a little more than milk-warm, add it slowly to the beaten yolks and sugar; then add flour and whites of the eggs; stir all together and throw in thin slices of good sour apples, dipping the batter up over them; drop into boiling hot lard in large spoonfuls with pieces of apple in each, and fry to a light brown. Serve with maple syrup or a nice syrup made with clarified sugar.

Bananas, peaches, sliced oranges and other fruits can be used in the same batter.

Baked Apple Dumplings

5 medium apples	1 tablespoon flour
1 recipe rich biscuit dough	1 teaspoon vinegar
Butter	1 tablespoon butter
Brown sugar	2 cups boiling water
1 cup brown sugar (firmly packed)	

Prepare the biscuit dough and roll to 1/4 inch thick, cut in 7 1/2 inch squares. Wash and core apples and place one in the center of the dough. Fill center of apple with brown sugar and top with butter. Bring dough up around apple and press together. Put these dumplings in a buttered baking dish. Combine brown sugar, flour, vinegar and butter in saucepan, add boiling water, mix and boil 2 minutes. Pour half of this syrup over the dumplings and put in a hot oven (400°) for 40 minutes or until apples are tender. Heat the remaining syrup to serve with dumplings.

Baked Indian Pudding

(100 year-old recipe)

4 cups milk	1 egg, beaten	1 cup molasses
3 large tablespoons corn meal	1 teaspoon salt	
1 teaspoon ginger	1 teaspoon vanilla	
1 tablespoon butter		

Scald three cups of milk. Mix the egg, beaten, molasses, one cup of cold milk and corn meal, and remaining ingredients. Add to the scalded milk and cook over hot water until thick. Pour into baking dish and bake in slow oven two hours. Serve with cream or hard sauce.

Old-Fashioned Apple Dumpling

(Cooked in Boiling Water)

1 quart flour	1 tablespoon butter
1½ teaspoons baking powder	2 cups milk
½ teaspoon salt	Large tart apples
1 tablespoon shortening	Sugar

Sift the flour twice with the baking powder and salt. Chop into this the shortening and butter. Mix into a soft dough with the milk; roll out into a sheet a scant half inch thick, and cut into squares about five inches in size. Lay in the center of each a large, tart apple, pared and cored. Fill the space left by coring with sugar; fold the corners of the dough together, enveloping the apple, tie up in cheesecloth squares dipped into hot water and well floured on the inside. Have ready a pot of boiling water. Drop in the dumplings and cook fast for one hour. Dip each for one second in cold water to loosen the cloth, turn out upon a hot dish and serve with hard sauce or lemon sauce.

46

Sailor Duff

1 egg	½ cup boiling water
2 tablespoons sugar	1½ cups flour (scant)
½ cup molasses	1 tablespoon melted fat
1 teaspoon soda	

Beat egg, add sugar and molasses. Dissolve soda in boiling water and add to mixture, alternately with flour; add butter. Beat well and steam one hour in individual molds. Serve with St. Cecilia Sauce.

ST. CECILIA SAUCE

Beat 2 egg yolks and add gradually, while still beating, one cup of powdered sugar. Fold in one cup of heavy cream (whipped), and flavor with one tablespoon of sherry.

Blueberry Dumplings

2 cups blueberries	1 cup sugar
3 tablespoons lemon juice	2 cups water
Grated rind 1 lemon	¼ teaspoon salt
¼ teaspoon cinnamon, optional	

Wash the blueberries and combine with lemon juice, rind, sugar, water, salt, and cinnamon in a saucepan. Cook for 4 or 5 minutes. While the mixture cooks, prepare the following batter.

DUMPLINGS

1 cup sifted all-purpose flour	½ cup sugar
2 teaspoons baking powder	2 tablespoons butter
¼ teaspoon salt	½ cup milk

Cream the butter and sugar; add the milk; then mix in the flour which has been sifted with the baking powder and salt. Drop this batter by spoonfuls into the boiling blueberry mixture. Cover and boil gently over low heat for 20 minutes without removing cover.

Blueberry dumplings are a real old-fashioned dessert to serve with a topping of cream or ice cream.

Steamed Blueberry Puff

2 cups all-purpose flour   1 teaspoon salt
2 teaspoons baking powder   1½ cups milk

Sift flour, baking powder and salt together. Add milk, mix well. This should make a soft batter. Butter molds (individual) and place them on a steamer rack. Place a spoonful of batter then a spoonful of berries in each mold until two-thirds full. Steam 25 minutes. Serve with blueberry sauce.

Fresh Blueberry Pie

1 quart fresh blueberries   1 tablespoon butter
1 cup granulated sugar   ⅛ teaspoon salt
2 tablespoons flour or 1½ tablespoons quick cooking tapioca
1 to 2 teaspoons lemon juice   ½ teaspoon cinnamon (optional

Combine sugar, flour and salt (also cinnamon if you desire). Place half of berries in pie plate lined with pastry; sprinkle with half of sugar mixture. Repeat. Dot with butter. Place on top crust Bake at 425° F. until crust is nicely browned and filling begins to bubble. Lower temperature to 350° F. to complete cooking.

Molasses Blueberry Cake

2 eggs

1 cup sugar

½ cup molasses

½ cup shortening

1 cup sour milk (or hot water may be used instead)

3 scant cups flour

1 teaspoon baking soda

2 cups blueberries (washed, drained, and floured)

1 teaspoon each of nutmeg, cloves, cinnamon and allspice

Bake in greased and lightly floured pan in 350° oven, baking time depends on size pan used.

Submitted by Mrs. Milton Grierson, South Thomaston, Maine

Blueberry Cottage Pudding

Make cottage pudding recipe in cupcake tins. Serve with blueberry sauce poured over the individual puddings and accompany with a slice of hard sauce generously sprinkled with nutmeg.

For the stewed blueberry sauce cook together in a saucepan 2 cups blueberries, ¼ cup water, ½ cup sugar, ¼ teaspoon cinnamon and 1 tablespoon butter. Simmer gently 10 minutes.

Old-Fashioned Steamed Apple Pudding

2 cups flour	¾ to 1 cup milk
4 teaspoons baking powder	4 apples, pared, cut in eighths
1 teaspoon salt (scant)	1 tablespoon sugar
2 tablespoons shortening	¼ teaspoon cinnamon or nutmeg

Mix the first five ingredients as for baking powder biscuits. Roll out the dough, spread the apples on it, sprinkling with the tablespoon of sugar and ¼ teaspoon of cinnamon. Roll up the dough and apples as for jelly roll and place in a buttered steaming mold with a tight cover; or one may use a three pound shortening can covered. If you do not have a cover use two or three sheets of waxpaper, covering carefully. Put mold in some water in a covered kettle and steam for 1½ hours. This is delicious served with the molasses sauce recipe, given under pudding sauces. One may prefer vanilla or lemon pudding sauce.

STEAMED BLUEBERRY PUDDING

Follow the same recipe as above substituting ¾ cup blueberries and ½ cup sugar for the apples and sugar in steamed apple pudding. Serve with cream or hard sauce.

Submitted by Mrs. Inez Montgomery, Owls Head, Maine

Golden Ball Fritters (1850)

Put into a stewpan a pint of water, a piece of butter as large as an egg and a tablespoonful of sugar. When it boils stir into it one pint of sifted flour, stirring briskly and thoroughly. Remove from the fire, and when nearly cooled beat into it six eggs, each one beaten separately and added one at a time, beating the batter between each. Drop the stiff dough into boiling lard by teaspoonfuls. Eat with syrup, or melted sugar and butter flavored.

Stirring the boiling lard around and around, so that it whirls when you drop in the fritters, causes them to assume a round shape like balls.

Molasses Apple Pan Dowdy

5 or 6 tart apples	1/2 teaspoon mace
1/2 cup water	1/2 teaspoon salt
1/2 cup molasses	2 cups all purpose flour
3/4 cup sugar	4 teaspoons baking powder
3 tablespoons butter	1/2 teaspoon salt
3 tablespoons corn starch	1/3 cup shortening
2/3 cup milk	

Pare, core and slice apples in wedges into a buttered baking dish, 8 x 13 x 2 inches. Add water and cook in the oven a few minutes until soft. In a saucepan mix the molasses, sugar, corn starch, mace, and salt. Boil together until thoroughly blended. Pour this mixture over the apples. Mix and sift flour, baking powder and salt in bowl, cut in fat as for biscuits, add milk and mix. Roll this dough to 1/4 inch thick and cut with 2 1/2 inch biscuit cutter. Place biscuits over the molasses mixture. Bake at 425° until biscuits are brown. Many prefer pie crust topping.

Cottage Pudding

1/4 cup shortening	2 1/4 cups flour
2/3 cup sugar	4 teaspoons baking powder
1 egg	1 teaspoon vanilla
1 cup milk	1/2 teaspoon salt

Cream shortening, add sugar and vanilla, then well beaten egg. Mix and sift flour, baking powder and salt and add alternately with milk to first mixture. Turn into a greased cake pan. Bake at 350°F. or pour into greased individual molds and steam 1 hour. Serve with lemon, chocolate or quick raspberry cream sauce.

Rice Butterscotch Pudding

2 tablespoons gelatine	2 cups scalded milk
¼ cup cold water	1 cup cooked rice
¼ cup butter	1 cup cream, whipped
1 cup brown sugar	1 teaspoon vanilla

Soak the gelatine in the cold water. In the meantime, melt the butter in a saucepan and stir in one cup of brown sugar; cook slowly until well blended. Add the scalded milk and cook until the sugar is thoroughly dissolved. While the mixture is very hot, add the gelatine and stir it until it is dissolved. Cool, and when the mixture begins to congeal, add one cup of cooked rice and one cup of cream, whipped. Flavor with one teaspoon of vanilla. Pour into a mould and let chill until thoroughly firm. Serve with Salted Pecan Sauce.

SALTED PECAN SAUCE

2 cups brown sugar	2 cups cold water
2 tablespoons flour	1 teaspoon vanilla
¼ cup butter	1 cup salted pecans, chopped

In a saucepan, mix the brown sugar, flour, butter and cold water. Cook until a thick syrup is obtained, remove from the heat, flavor with vanilla and add salted pecans. Cool, and serve over the pudding.

Jackson Pudding

1 quart milk	½ cup sugar
½ cup rice	3 eggs

Boil the rice in milk until well cooked, beat the yolks of eggs and add sugar, salt and flavoring to rice. Dash of salt and 1 teaspoon of vanilla. Cook a minute then pour into an ovenproof dish. Beat the whites of eggs with 6 tablespoons of sugar to stiff froth, pour over the pudding, brown in oven, set to cool.

Submitted by Mrs. J. Warren Everett, Thomaston, Maine

Blanc-Mange Made with Sea Moss

1 quart milk	3 tablespoons sugar
1 tablespoon sea moss farina	1 teaspoon vanilla
½ teaspoon salt	

Put milk in double boiler and sprinkle sea moss into it, stirring all the while. Heat slowly. Stir often. When it boils up and looks white, add sugar, salt and flavor. Strain and turn into mold which has been dipped in cold water. It takes 3 hours to harden.

Handed down from the Captain of the Packet Clara Belle,
Winterport to Deer Isle

Grapenut Pudding

4 egg yolks, well beaten	½ cup butter	2 cups sugar
Juice and grated rind of 2 lemons		4 tablespoons flour
6 tablespoons grapenuts		4 egg-whites, beaten stiff
2 cups milk		

Cream butter and sugar thoroughly, add egg yolks, flour, grapenuts, milk, lemon juice and rind. Fold in the egg whites. Pour into a greased baking dish, place it in a pan of hot water. Bake in a moderate oven (350°F.) for 50 to 60 minutes. When done, the pudding will have a crust on top and jelly below. Serve hot or cold with plain or whipped cream.

Baked Apple Tapioca Pudding

6 or 8 large red tart apples, pared, cored and sliced	
2/3 cup sugar	3 cups water
1/3 cup minute tapioca	2 tablespoons butter
1 teaspoon vanilla	

Put the sliced apples in a buttered baking dish (not glass) with 1½ cups water and the 2 tablespoons of butter. Cook until light and fluffy. Mix sugar, minute tapioca, vanilla with 3 cups water and cook in double broiler until clear. Take from stove and pour over apples in baking dish. Put in slow oven (300 degrees) and cook for 2 hours, stirring occasionally. This should be a dark pink and quite thick when done. Serve cold with whipped cream, chopped nuts and a sprinkling of cinnamon.

Taken from an old cook book.

Cabinet Pudding

(100 Year Old Recipe)

1 quart milk	1 tablespoon butter
4 eggs	3 pints stale sponge or plain cake
4 tablespoons sugar	1 cup raisins
½ teaspoon salt	

Beat the eggs, sugar and salt together, and add the milk. Butter a three-pint pudding mold, sprinkle the sides and bottom with the fruit, and put in a layer of cake. Again sprinkle in fruit, and put in more cake. Continue this until all the materials are used. Gradually pour on the custard. Let the pudding stand two hours, and steam an hour and a quarter. Serve with cream sauce.

Judge Peters Pudding

¾ box of gelatine	6 figs
2 cups sugar	9 dates
2 lemons	2 bananas
2 oranges	10 walnuts

Dissolve the gelatine in ½ pint cold water for one hour. Then add ½ pint boiling water, the juice of the lemons and the sugar. Strain and let stand until it begins to thicken. Stir into this all the fruit cut into small pieces. Pour into a mold and let harden. Serve with whipped cream.

Bread and Butter Pudding

(Over 100 Years Old)

Cut in thin slices a baker's five-cent loaf, wash and pick over 1 cup of currants. Butter each slice of bread. Put a layer of this bread in the bottom of a one-quart mold or basin, then a sprinkling of currants, and so on until all is used. Beat 4 eggs and a half cup of sugar together until light; add gradually 1 pint of milk, and a quarter of a nutmeg, grated. Pour this over the bread, let stand 15 minutes and bake in a moderate oven 30 minutes. Serve cold with Cream Sauce.

CREAM SAUCE

One teacup powdered white sugar, scant half teacup butter, half teacup rich cream; beat butter and sugar thoroughly, add cream, stir the whole into half teacup boiling water, place on stove for a few moments, stirring it constantly; take off, and add flavoring.

Fruit Cake

1 cup cold water	1 teaspoon cinnamon
1 cup brown sugar	1 cup raisins
1/3 cup shortening	2 cups flour
½ teaspoon cloves	1 teaspoon soda

Combine cold water, brown sugar, shortening, cloves, cinnamon, and raisins in a saucepan, and bring to a boil. Cool. Add the flour and soda. Bake in a slow oven (300 degrees) for at least 1 hour. Add any other fruit desired. Keeps a week.

Submitted by Mattie Campbell, Warren, Maine

Butterscotch Apple Tapioca

2 large, tart apples	1½ tablespoon lemon juice
2 cups water	2/3 cup light brown sugar
1/3 cup quick-cooking tapioca	½ teaspoon salt
2 tablespoons butter	

Peel, core and slice the apples. Place in a shallow buttered baking dish. Pour over the water and lemon juice and cook half an hour at 350°F.

In the meantime, combine the tapioca and one-half cup sugar and salt. Stir into the apple mixture and cook 15 minutes longer. Sprinkle the remaining sugar over the top, and dot with the butter. Return to oven for 5 minutes. Serve with hard sauce.

Steamed Chocolate Pudding

Cream ½ cup sugar with 1 tablespoon butter, add 1 beaten egg and ½ cup sweet milk. Sift 1 cup flour with 1 teaspoon cream of tartar, ½ teaspoon soda, and salt, add to first mixture with 2 squares of melted chocolate. Pour into greased and floured tin or mold— steam 1½ hours. Serve with hard sauce or whipped cream.

HARD SAUCE

¼ cup butter creamed   ⅛ teaspoon salt
¾ cup confectioners' sugar   1 teaspoon vanilla

Cream well together, form in a roll or small pats, chill in refrigerator. Slice the roll and serve on hot pudding.

Submitted by Miss Etta F. Beverage, North Haven, Maine

Rice Pudding

(100 Year Old Recipe)

1 cup rice   2 eggs, separated
2 cups milk   ½ cup sugar
1 teaspoon corn starch   Juice and grated rind of 1 lemon
1 cup raisins (optional)   4 tablespoons sugar

To a cup of rice boiled in a custard kettle in a pint of water (seasoned with salt) until dry, add a pint of milk in which the corn starch has been dissolved, and boil again; add the yolks of 2 eggs beaten with ½ cup of sugar, stir well together, and lastly add the juice and grated rind of 1 lemon. Place in a dish, and bake slowly in the oven (300°F.); when done spread over the top the whites beaten with 4 tablespoons sugar, and brown in oven.

VARIATIONS

1. A cup of raisins may be added just before baking.

2. After boiling the rice with the milk, eggs and sugar, add a lump of butter and place a layer of the rice, about an inch thick, in a buttered dish sprinkled with bread crumbs, then a layer of peaches (either fresh or canned), repeat until dish is full, leaving rice for the last layer; bake slowly for half an hour, and when done, cover with the beaten whites, as above.

3. Or, after preparing the rice as above, add pineapple, chopped fine, or oranges or dried cherries; mix thoroughly, and bake and finish as above.

Dried Apple Fruit Cake

(Over 100 Years Old)

Soak three cupfuls of dried apples overnight in cold water enough to swell them, in the morning put them on the fire with three cups of molasses; stew until almost soft; add a cupful of nice raisins (seedless, if possible) and stew a few moments; when cold, add three cupfuls of flour, one cupful of butter, three eggs and a teaspoonful of soda; bake in a steady oven. This will make two good-sized panfuls of splendid cake; the apples will cook like citron and taste deliciously. Raisins may be omitted; also spices to taste may be added. This is not a dear but a delicious cake.

Rhubarb Custard Pie

1 cup stewed rhubarb   2 egg yolks, beaten
1¼ cups sugar   1 cup milk

Mix together and pour into unbaked pie shell. Beat the whites and fold into custard with fork. Bake at 350 degrees until custard is set.

Submitted by Mrs. Flora Turner, Washington, Maine

Lemon Pie with Two Crusts

(100 Year Old Recipe)

1 lemon, juice and grated rind   1 cup sugar
2 eggs   1 teaspoon corn starch
1 teaspoon butter   1 cup milk

Beat lemon, sugar and eggs together for ten minutes. Rub the butter and corn starch. Mix thoroughly with the other ingredients. Add the milk. Water can be substituted if milk is not convenient. Stir until well mixed. Pour into a deep pie pan lined with crust and cover with a top crust. Wet the edges of the pie crust and press tightly together. Bake quickly.

Easy Lemon Meringue Pie

1 cup sugar
1/3 cup corn starch (scant)
2 cups hot water

1/3 cup lemon juice
4 egg yolks

Combine all ingredients, in the order given, in the top of a double boiler. Cook until thick, stirring constantly to prevent lumping. Do not beat with an egg beater as this will keep the pie from setting. Place in a baked pie shell. Top with meringue.

MERINGUE

3 egg whites (room temperature)
¼ teaspoon cream of tartar
6 tablespoons sugar

Few grains of salt
½ teaspoon vanilla (optional)

Beat egg whites (at room temperature give a larger volume than cold egg whites) until just foamy throughout, add cream of tartar and salt. Beat just to blend well. Add sugar, 1 tablespoon at a time, beating well after each addition. Continue beating until stiff and glossy — about 5 minutes.

Pile meringue onto hot pie filling, being careful to seal the meringue onto the edge of crust to prevent shrinking and weeping. Swirl meringue with back of spoon to make peaks.

Bake 12 to 15 minutes in a 350°F. oven until meringue is lightly browned. Cool on wire rack, away from drafts, until bottom of pie is at room temperaure. To serve, dip knife or pie server in water after making each cut.

Pineapple Sponge Pie

1 cup sugar
2 egg yolks

2 heaping teaspoons flour
Melted butter size of an egg

Mix well together and add 1 cup crushed pineapple and 1 cup milk, fold in 2 stiffly beaten egg whites. Pour into uncooked crust and bake slowly 30 minutes. The custard will remain at the bottom and the sponge mixture will be on top when baked.

Submitted by Miss Rosamond Danforth, Union, Maine

Bakers' Custard Pie

(Old-Time Recipe)

Beat up the yolks of three eggs to a cream. Stir thoroughly a tablespoonful of sifted flour into three tablespoonfuls of sugar; this separates the particles of flour so that there will be no lumps; then add it to the beaten yolks, put in a pinch of salt, a teaspoonful of vanilla and a little grated nutmeg; next the well beaten whites of the eggs; and lastly, a pint of scalded milk (not boiled) which has been cooled; mix this in by degrees and turn all into a deep pie pan lined with paste, and bake in a 425° F. oven from 25 to 30 minutes.

(This recipe was received from a celebrated cook in one of the best New York bakeries — the secret to the look of solidity and smoothness is the addition of this bit of flour — not that it thickens the custard any to speak of, but prevents the custard from breaking or wheying and gives that smooth appearance when cut.)

My Lemon Pie

(Original Recipe)

1½ cups sugar   1½ cups cold water
2/3 cup flour   Yolks of 3 eggs
¼ teaspoon salt
1/3 cup lemon juice, and grated rinds of the lemons

Mix together the sugar, flour and salt and add the water and lemon juice, also the egg yolks. Beat well and cook in double boiler until thick, then add the lemon rind and a piece of butter the size of an egg. Pour into an unbaked pie shell and bake in a 450 degree oven until the crust has cooked. Add meringue made of the whites of the three eggs and bake at 325 degrees for 20 minutes or until the meringue is brown.

MERINGUE

Whites of 3 eggs   Pinch of salt
1/3 cup sugar   ½ teaspoon baking powder

Beat the whites of eggs stiff, add one-half of the sugar, the salt, and beat again until well mixed. Next fold in the rest of the sugar and the baking powder. This meringue never fails and is always a perfect one.

Submitted by Mrs. Percy E. Demmons, Thomaston, Maine

Grandma Nancy's Lemon Cake

(An 1850 Recipe)

1 cup butter	4 cups flour
3 cups sugar	1 cup milk
5 egg yolks	4 egg whites, beaten stiff
1 large lemon, grated peel and juice	
½ teaspoon saleratus (soda)	

Cream butter and add gradually while still creaming the sugar. Beat the egg yolks until thick and lemon colored; add to the first mixture. Flavor with the grated peel and juice of the large lemon. Sift the soda with the flour and stir lightly into the mixture alternately with the milk. Beat the four egg whites until stiff and fold into the mixture. Pour the cake batter into two well buttered loaf pans, 11 x 4 x 3 inches deep. Bake at 325 - 350°F. for about 50 minutes. Remove the cake from pan. Cool. Dust the top lightly with confectioners' sugar.

Baked Lemon Pudding

(Queen of Puddings — From An 1887 Cook Book)

One quart of milk, 2 cupfuls of bread crumbs, four eggs, white and yolks beaten separately, butter the size of an egg, one cupful of white sugar, one large lemon — juice and grated rind. Heat the milk and pour over the bread crumbs, add the butter, cover and let it get soft. When cool, beat the sugar and yolks and add to the mixture, also the grated rind. Bake in a buttered dish until firm and slightly brown, from a half to three-quarters of an hour. When done, draw it to the door of the oven and cover with a meringue made of the whites of the eggs, whipped to a froth with four tablespoonfuls of powdered sugar and the lemon juice; put it back in the oven and brown a light straw color. Eat warm, with lemon sauce.

Molasses Filled Cookies

1 egg
1 cup sugar
1 cup molasses
Fill cup ¾ full of soft lard and finish filling with boiling water
1 tablespoon vinegar
1 teaspoon ginger   ½ teaspoon salt
1 heaping teaspoon soda   Flour to make a very stiff dough

FILLING

1 pound dates cut up   Water to almost cover
2 tablespoons sugar

Cook, stirring constantly until it thickens which will be only a few minutes.

The first part of the above cookies is very delicious rolled out and used without the filling. It also keeps well. It is an old-fashioned recipe which came from Canada.

Submitted by Mrs. Amy Stebbins, Bath, Maine

Soft Molasses Cookies

1 cup sugar   2 tablespoons vinegar
1 cup bacon fat (melted)   2 tablespoons water (cold)
1 cup molasses   2 teaspoons baking soda
2 eggs   ¼ teaspoon each of ginger, cloves and cinnamon
Add 4 cups flour. Mix well. Roll out ¼ inch thick. Bake in oven 375° for 10 minutes.

Submitted by Mrs. Harmon Reed, Thomaston, Maine

Molasses Doughnuts

½ cup molasses   1 teaspoon soda
¼ cup sugar   ½ teaspoon ginger
½ cup sour milk   1 teaspoon salt
1 egg   ½ teaspoon nutmeg or cassia
2 cups flour or just enough to handle easily
Fry in hot fat (380°). Turn once. Makes 24.

Monhegan Island Doughnuts

3 tablespoons melted butter
1½ cups sugar
2 eggs
1 cup buttermilk
4 cups flour

3 teaspoons baking powder
½ teaspoon baking soda
1 teaspoon salt
1 teaspoon nutmeg
½ teaspoon cinnamon

Combine first four ingredients and beat until light. Sift dry ingredients and add. Stir in well, then pour on floured board and knead until smooth — roll ¼ inch thick and cut out. Fry at 380°. Turn once. Makes 36.

Chocolate Doughnuts

2 eggs
1 teaspoon salt
1½ teaspoons soda
3 cups flour
1 cup sugar

3 squares chocolate
1½ tablespoons melted butter
1 cup sour milk
1 teaspoon vanilla

Beat eggs, sugar, butter, chocolate (melted) and sour milk together — add 2 cups flour in which soda has been sifted — then stir in rest of flour. Knead on floured board. Roll to ¼ inch thick, cut with 3 inch cutter. Fry at 325°. Makes 30.

Raised Doughnuts

1 cup milk
1 yeast cake softened in ¼ cup lukewarm water
1 teaspoon salt
3½ cups flour
3 tablespoons butter
2 tablespoons other shortening

1 cup sugar
2 eggs, well beaten
½ teaspoon nutmeg

Scald milk, cool to lukewarm. Add salt and 2 cups flour. Let rise ½ hour. Melt butter and other shortening. Add dough with sugar, eggs, nutmeg and 1½ cups flour. Let rise until light, punch down. Turn out on floured board, add more flour if too soft to knead. Roll about ½ inch thick, cut with 3 inch doughnut cutter. Let rise on board 1 hour. Fry at 380°.

Dip each doughnut in thin confectioners frosting and place on cake rack over waxpaper until it sets. Place on towel and cover with towel when cooled. This will prevent them from getting sticky. Makes 24.

Blueberry Muffins

To the regular recipe for plain muffins fold in two-thirds cup of fresh or frozen blueberries. If some sugar and a little cinnamon are added to the blueberries and stirred quickly into the muffins, a very good flavor results.

Potato Flour Muffins

4 eggs, separated	½ cup potato flour
½ teaspoon salt	1 teaspoon baking powder
1 tablespoon sugar	2 tablespoons ice water

Beat the yolks of four eggs until lemon colored; beat in one-half a teaspoon salt. Beat the whites of four eggs with one tablespoon of sugar until stiff. Sift together, three times, one-half a cup of potato flour and one teaspoon of baking powder, and fold into the beaten whites. Fold the two egg mixtures together, when smooth, fold in two tablespoons of ice water. Bake in a muffin pan in a moderate oven twenty minutes.

Aunt Mame's Muffins

Soak 2 cups of rolled oats in
1½ cups of sour milk (not too sour) until soft
1 cup of flour (any kind)
1 egg
3 Tbsp. melted shortening
3 mixing spoons molasses (1/3 cup)
1¾ teaspoon soda
½ teaspoon salt

Bake in 375 degree oven for 25 minutes. Makes 1½ dozen. Better served cold than hot.

Aunt Datie's Squash Muffins

4 tablespoons mashed squash
¾ cup milk
½ cup sugar
½ teaspoon salt

2 cups flour
5 teaspoon baking powder
3 tablespoons melted butter

Blend squash with sugar, add the salt and baking powder to flour that has been sifted and measured. Add milk and melted butter to squash and sugar, sift in dry ingredients and blend. Bake in 375 degree oven 15 to 20 minutes.

Doughnut Muffins

1/3 cup shortening
1 cup sugar
1 egg
1½ cups flour

1½ teaspoons baking powder
½ teaspoon salt
¼ teaspoon nutmeg
½ cup milk

Cream sugar and shortening, add egg beaten. Sift dry ingredients and add alternately with milk. Bake 20 to 30 minutes at 350 degrees. Remove from pan and roll in 6 tablespoons melted butter or oleo, then roll in ½ cup sugar and 1 teaspoon cinnamon mixture.

Brown Bread

1 cup corn meal
1 cup rye or graham flour
1 cup white flour
1 cup molasses

2 cups sour milk or hot water
1 teaspoon soda
1 teaspoon salt

Mix dry ingredients, then add molasses and sour milk or hot water. Raisins may be added. Steam in greased dish, covered for 5 hours.

Johnny Cake

2 cups corn meal
1 cup flour
1 teaspoon salt

1 pint sour milk with 2 teaspoons soda
1½ tablespoons molasses

Combine in order given and bake in 450 degree oven 15 minutes.

Baking Powder Biscuits

(In The 1800's)

One quart of flour sifted two or three times, two heaping teaspoonfuls of baking powder, a pinch of salt, and one tablespoonful of lard mixed thoroughly through the flour. Then pour in one-half pint of cream or cream and water; do not knead much, but roll out on the board; double the dough and roll again, repeating this once or twice. Do not touch the hands to it any more than necessary; cut into biscuits; make them touch each other in the pan. You will have delicious biscuits with very little trouble.

Buttermilk Biscuits

2 cups flour	½ teaspoon baking soda
1 tablespoon baking powder	3 tablepsoons shortening
½ teaspoon salt	¾ cup buttermilk
½ teaspoon sugar	

Mix and sift first four ingredients. Add shortening and mix with pastry blender. Add buttermilk to which baking soda has been added (stir in). Stir together to make ball of dough. Pour out on floured board and knead three times. Cut with biscuit cutter. Bake at 475 degrees for 15 minutes.

Cream of Tartar Biscuits

2 cups flour	½ teaspoon salt
5 teaspoons cream of tartar	5 tablespoons shortening
2 teaspoons soda	¾ cup milk

Sift dry ingredients, add shortening, blend with fork or pastry blender. Add milk and stir together. Pour onto board and knead 5 or 6 times. Cut out with small biscuit cutter. Bake at 475° 12 to 15 minutes. (5 teaspoons of Cream of Tartar is correct).

Bakewell Cream Biscuits

4 cups flour	1 teaspoon salt
4 teaspoon Bakewell Cream	½ cup shortening
2 teaspoons soda	1½ cups milk

Mix and sift first four ingredients. Add shortening and mix with pastry blender. Add milk all at once and stir quickly together with a fork to make a soft dough (some flours require more liquid, so add more milk if your dough seems too stiff). Pour out on floured board and knead 5 or 6 times. Roll out ½ inch or more thick. Cut with biscuit cutter. Top each with a little milk or bit of butter. Bake at 475 degrees for 5 minutes, then turn off heat and bake until golden brown.

(Bakewell Cream is a high quality cream tartar substitute. If you cannot find it in your grocery store, it is packed by Byron H. Smith & Co., Bangor, Me.)

These biscuits are extra high and light.

Squash Biscuits

1 cup squash (seasoned for table)	2 tablespoons sour cream
1 teaspoon soda	1 teaspoon salt
1 cup sour milk	2 cups flour

Mix dry ingredients and sift. Add milk and cream, stir. Pour on board, add more flour if necessary to knead like other biscuits. Cut out. Bake twelve minutes at 450 degrees.

Loaf Bread and Rolls

1 cup milk	6 cups flour
2 tablespoons sugar	1 package yeast or
2 teaspoons salt	1 cake of compressed
2 tablespoons shortening	1 cup lukewarm water

Scald milk, add sugar, salt and shortening. Set aside to cool. Add yeast to lukewarm water, when milk is lukewarm combine the two. Sift and measure flour. Add flour gradually, stirring in well. When dough is moderately stiff, turn out onto floured board. Cover and let stand a few minutes. Knead until dough is satiny smooth. Make into ball and place in greased bowl. Cover and let rise in warm place until double in bulk. Punch down and divide into two equal parts. Let stand on lightly floured board a few minutes. Then pat one ball into loaf size for bread pan, pat down into corners of pan — let rise until doubled in size. Bake at 400 degrees 35 minutes. The rest of dough may be used for rolls. Soft rolls are made by packing them close together in 2 or 3 inch deep pan. Harder rolls by placing them well apart on cookie sheet. These may also be shaped into a variety of shapes such as clover leaf, bow knots, Crescents, fan-tan or others.

FROGS — a "Downeast Treat" are made by pinching off bits of raw bread dough and dropping into hot doughnut fat until brown. Serve with maple syrup and hot coffee.

Elsa's Coffee Bread

1 cup oleo (½ pound)
½ teaspoon salt
1¼ to 1 1/3 cups milk
1 cup sugar
6 level cups flour
2 yeast packages
¼ cup lukewarm water
7 eggs – 5 egg yolks and 2 whole eggs, all unbeaten
1 teaspoon cardiman seed (10-12 pods)

Place the yeast in the lukewarm water and set aside. Scald the milk, add the oleo, salt and sugar. When lukewarm, add the dissolved yeast, 5 egg yolks and the 2 whole eggs. Beat well. Beat in the flour and cardiman seed and knead well.

Place dough in large bowl, covering well with melted shortening and let rise, covered, until doubled. Punch down, cover, and put in refrigerator overnight.

In the morning, work with the cold dough. Divide the dough in 4 equal parts for making 4 braids. For each braid divide the dough in three strips and braid loosely, tucking ends under. Place on greased baking sheet. Brush with oleo or butter. Cover and let rise until double. Bake at 350°F. about 20 minutes.

While still warm frost with quick white icing: Sift 2 cups confectioners' sugar. Moisten with 2 tablespoons water, milk or 2 tablespoons cream to spread. Add 1 teaspoon vanilla. This dough may also be used for rolls which are delicious.

Submitted by Mrs. Elsa Kigel, Warren

Index

BEVERAGES

BREADS

CANDIES

CAMPERS' AND HUNTERS' SPECIALS

DESSERTS

Cake and Cookies

Doughnuts

Pies

Puddings

DRESSINGS

FISH
Seafoods and Fresh Water

MAIN DISHES

MISCELLANEOUS DISHES

PICKLES AND JAMS

SAUCES

Meat and Fish Sauces

Pudding Sauces

STUFFINGS

EQUIVALENTS

60 drops *equals* 1 teaspoon

3 teaspoons *equals* 1 tablespoon

16 tablespoons *equals* 1 cup

2 tablespoons *equals* 1 fluid ounce

4 tablespoons *equals* ¼ cup

1 cup *equals* 8 fluid ounces

2 cups *equals* 1 pint

4 quarts *equals* 1 gallon

2 pints *equals* 1 quart

8 quarts *equals* 1 peck

4 pecks *equals* 1 bushel

2 cups liquid *equals* 1 pound

4 cups flour *equals* 1 pound

2 cups sugar *equals* 1 pound

2 2/3 cups brown sugar *equals* 1 pound

3½ cups powdered sugar *equals* 1 pound

2 cups butter *equals* 1 pound

16 ounces (dry measure) *equals* 1 pound

½ cup *equals* 1 gill

1 square *equals* 1 ounce chocolate

3 tablespoons cocoa plus ½ tablespoon butter *equals* 1 ounce chocolate

1 tablespoon corn starch (for thickening) *equals* 2 tablespoons flour

2 teaspoons baking powder *equals* 1 teaspoon cream of tartar and ½ teaspoon soda; or 2 cups sour or buttermilk with 1 teaspoon soda

1 egg *equals* 2 tablespoons flour for thickening

1 whole egg *equals* 2 egg yolks plus 1 tablespoon water (in cookies, etc.)

1 whole egg *equals* 2 egg yolks (in custards and such mixtures)

1 cup sour milk or buttermilk *equals* 1 cup fresh milk with 1 tablespoon lemon juice or vinegar stirred together

1 cup honey *equals* ¾ cup sugar plus ¼ cup liquid

Raisin Bread

1 cup milk

1/3 cup shortening

¾ cup sugar (for dough)

1 cup warm water

2 packages dry yeast (or 2 cakes fresh yeast)

6½ to 7 cups sifted all-purpose flour

2 teaspoons salt

2 cups seedless raisins (lightly floured)

1/3 cup sugar (for filling)

2 teaspoons cinnamon

Scald milk and cool to lukewarm. Cream shortening and add sugar gradually, creaming well. Sprinkle yeast on water; let stand for five minutes; add to creamed mixture. Beat in 2 cups flour. Cover with clean towel, let rise in warm place until dough is light and bubbly. Stir down dough; add salt and floured raisins. Blend in enough of remaining flour to make a soft dough. Knead dough until smooth and elastic. Let rise in warm place until double in bulk; knead again and let rise once more. Turn the dough onto bread board and divide in two parts. With rolling pin flatten each piece into a rectangle and spread it with one-half the cinnamon sugar mixture. Roll up like jelly roll; press the seam to seal it; place loaf seam side down in greased bread pan 9 x 5 x 3. Make second loaf with other half of dough. Cover pans and let dough rise to the top of pans. Bake in 375 degree oven for 45 minutes.

This is a very sweet, moist bread — Mrs. Luthera B. Dawson, 6302 Central Avenue, Capitol Heights 27, Maryland (formerly from Maine).

Batter Breads

Batter breads are quick to make. They are easier to handle as they need no kneading. They are not as fine grained and their use is somewhat limited because of the liquid consistency of the mixture.

Basic Batter:

1 package yeast or 1 yeast cake
1¼ cups warm water
¼ cup sugar
1 teaspoon salt

3 tablespoons dry milk solids
½ cup melted shortening
2 eggs
4 cups sifted flour

Sprinkle yeast into warm water. Stir until dissolved. Add sugar, salt, 2 cups flour and dry milk solids. Stir to mix, then beat smooth. Beat in eggs, then cooled melted shortening. Add remaining flour. Beat until batter is shiny and smooth. Scrape down from sides of bowl. Cover and set to rise in warm place until double, about 1 hour. Stir down and drop by spoonfuls into greased pan or muffin tins. Sprinkle top with cinnamon, sugar, nuts or crumb topping. Bake 375 degrees 30 minutes.

Salad Dressing

½ cup sugar
2 heaping tablespoons flour
1 level tablespoon mustard
1 cup vinegar and 1 cup water mixed
1 egg yolk

1 teaspoon salt
¼ teaspoon pepper

Cook until thick. Add beaten egg white (beaten with ½ cup of cream).

From Rockport Congregational Church Cook Book
Sent in By Miss Lillian Marie Whitmore

French Dressing

1 pint vegetable or salad oil
1 pint vinegar
1½ cups confectioners' sugar

1 tablespoon dry mustard
1 tablespoon celery seed

Mix all ingredients together and place in a covered container. This is a nice tart dressing for a tossed salad and will keep a long time.

Submitted by Mrs. Etta Anderson, Rockland, Maine

Celery Seed Dressing

1 teaspoon celery seed

¼ cup vinegar

½ cup sugar

¾ teaspoon salt

¾ teaspoon dry mustard

2 teaspoons onion juice

1 cup salad oil

Heat 2 tablespoons vinegar with celery seed, cool, combine rest of vinegar, sugar, salt, mustard and onion. Dissolve sugar completely. Add oil 1 tablespoon at a time, beating well after each addition with an egg beater until a thick emulsion is formed. Add vinegar and celery seed mixture slowly. Especially good on fruit salad.

Italian Dressing

¾ cup salad oil

1/3 cup vinegar

2 cloves garlic, crushed

½ teaspoon salt

¼ teaspoon pepper

Combine all ingredients in a screw top jar. Shake well, chill.

Southwest Harbor French Dressing

½ cup salad oil

5 tablespoons vinegar

1 teaspoon sugar

1 teaspoon salt

Few grains of pepper

Combine in a bottle and shake well.

Mouthwatering Bread and Butter Pickles

1 quart sliced, unpeeled cucumbers

1 large onion, sliced

1 tablespoon salt

Mix and let stand 3 hours. Drain and add 1 tablespoon mixed whole spice, 1 cup sugar, and vinegar to almost cover. Bring to boiling point but do not cook. Can at once. They need not be air tight. Make only this quantity at once to insure crispness.

Submitted by Mrs. Florence Thompson, South Portland, Maine

Spiced Beets

One peck baby beets — larger ones may be used and cut up Cook until done then skin and place in jars.

2 quarts vingar   4 cups sugar
4 teaspoons pickling spice (with red peppers discarded)

Heat above ingredients to boiling. Stir well to dissolve sugar. Pour over hot beets in jars. Seal. Makes 8 pint jars.

Sweet Mixed Pickles

1 quart sliced cucumbers

1 quart small cucumbers, whole

1 quart small button onions

3 quarts green tomatoes, sliced

1 head of cauliflower cut up fine

1 bunch celery cut up fine

4 red sweet peppers cut fine

Let stand overnight. Drain and scald in weak vinegar. Drain again. And add: 1½ quarts of brown sugar, 1 bag of spice containing ½ teaspoon ginger, 1 teaspoon cloves, and 2 teaspoons cassia. Cover with strong vinegar. Cook 40 to 50 minutes. Remove spice and put into jars.

Submitted by Inez G. McKay, Portland, Maine

Snappy Cole Slaw

½ cup vinegar   ¼ teaspoon celery seed

1 tablespoon butter or oleo   ⅛ teaspoon black pepper

¼ cup sugar   ⅛ teaspoon paprika

½ teaspoon salt   ½ head cabbage, shredded

½ teaspoon dry mustard

Bring the vinegar and butter to a boil. Remove from heat and add all the other ingredients except the cabbage. Allow to cool and pour over the cabbage. Stir well. Serves 6.

To Pickle Eggs

(In 1894 Cook Book)

One dozen eggs, 1 quart of vinegar, one-half ounce of black pepper, one-half ounce of ginger; boil the eggs twelve minutes; dip in cold water and take off the shell; put the vinegar with the pepper and ginger into a stew pan and simmer ten minutes; place the eggs in a jar, pour over the seasoned vinegar boiling hot.

HINT: The correct method for cooking eggs to prevent them from discoloring is to use a deep saucepan and 2 cups of water for each egg. Have the water boiling, put in eggs, remove from heat and let stand 45 to 60 minutes. Or start in cold water, bring to a boil, remove from heat, let stand 20 to 30 minutes.

Sweet Whole Cukes

(100 Years Old)

1 gallon best cider vinegar	1 cup grated horseradish
1 scant cup salt	1 scant tablespoon alum
2 cups brown sugar	1 tablespoon mixed spices
1 cup ground mustard	

Wipe cucumbers and pack in crock or large jars. Pour mixture over them until they all are under vinegar. Seal or weigh down with plate.

Crabapple Pickles

(Well Over 100 Years Old)

1 gallon crab apples	1 stick cinnamon
8 cups sugar	1 tablespoon crushed ginger
3 cups water	1 tablespoon whole allspice
4 cups vinegar	½ tablespoon whole cloves

Wash and pierce the apples with a needle. Heat sugar, liquids, and spices (tied in bag) until sugar dissolves. Cool. Add apples, simmer until tender. Let stand overnight. Pack cold apples in hot jars. Bring syrup to boil and pour over apples. Process 5 minutes in hot bath.

Ripe Cuke Pickles

(Well Over 100 Years Old)

Peel large, ripe firm cucumbers, cut in quarters, scrape out seeds, soak in weak brine overnight (½ cup salt to 1 gallon water). Drain thoroughly and scald in clear boiling water. Make a syrup of 1 quart vinegar, 2 pounds sugar, 1 tablespoon whole allspice, 1 tablespoon whole cloves, 1 stick of cinnamon, and 1 tablespoon crushed ginger root. Combine and boil 5 minutes. Add cucumber pieces and cook until clear. Can in hot jars immediately.

Cucumber Ketchup

2 quarts ripe cucumbers	4 tablespoons mustard seed
2 cups onion	3 cups vinegar
4 green peppers	2 teaspoons cayenne pepper
2 cups sugar	Salt to taste

Pare, seed and chop vegetables. Add 1½ cups water and cook until tender (not soft). Add other ingredients and cook until thick. Pour into hot jars and seal at once. Good on hot dogs or hamburgers.

Heavenly Jam

3 pounds sugar	Juice and pulp of 2 oranges
3 pounds peaches	1 small bottle maraschino cherries and juice
Grated rind of 1 orange	

Mash peaches fine. Add sugar. Let stand overnight. In the morning add oranges, rind, pulp, and cherry juice. Cook slowly about 1 hour. Add cherries cut in fine pieces just before putting in jars

Submitted by Mrs. Florence Thompson, South Portland, Maine

Blueberry Conserve

2 quarts blueberries	1 orange
4 pounds granulated sugar	½ pound seeded raisins
1 lemon	

Put lemon, orange and raisins through meat grinder, then add to blueberries and sugar. Boil gently about 45 minutes or until it "jams" when cool. Add 1 cup chopped walnuts.

This is delicious with cold meats and delectable on thin pancakes, then topped with a dollop of sour cream.

Submitted by Mrs. Kenneth K. Stowell, Friendship, Maine

German Cabbage

Chop medium size cabbage. Cover with boiling water. Add one sliced onion. Add one-half teaspoon nutmeg. Cook for about 20 minutes or until tender. Drain off nearly all water. Add two tablespoons butter, two tablespoons vinegar, and one tablespoon sugar. Cook for five minutes longer.

Submitted by Mrs. Frederick C. Lewis, Rockland, Maine

Beet Salad

3 good size beets boiled or 1 large can. Pour 1½ cups of hot beet water and ½ cup vinegar over 1 package lemon jello, when slightly thickened add 1 cup diced beets and 2 tablespoons horseradish. Mold, cut in squares and serve on lettuce with salad dressing and a sprinkle of paprika.

Submitted by Ethel Colburn, Rockland, Maine

Harvard Beets

½ cup sugar   ½ tablespoon corn starch
¼ cup vinegar   Salt
½ cup water

Heat and cook until it thickens, and then add your freshly cooked beets, sliced or diced the way you like them. Let set ½ hour or so, reheat and add a piece of butter.

Submitted by Edna Dyer, North Haven, Maine

Spiced Plums (1894)

Make a syrup, allowing one pound of sugar to one of plums, and to every three pounds of sugar a scant pint of vinegar. Allow one ounce each of ground cinnamon, cloves, mace, and allspice to a peck of plums. Prick the plums. Add the spices to the syrup, and pour, boiling, over the plums. Let these stand three days; then skim them out, and boil down the syrup until it is quite thick, and pour hot over the plums in the jar in which they are to be kept. Cover closely. Let stand three days.

Lemon Pudding Sauce

1½ tablespoons corn starch
1 cup boiling water
3 tablespoons lemon juice
½ cup sugar

1 teaspoon grated lemon rind
1 tablespoon butter
Few grains of salt
Nutmeg

Blend the corn starch and sugar, add the water and cook 15 minutes, stirring constantly until thick. Add the lemon juice and rind and the butter. Serves 6. For Vanilla Sauce, omit lemon and add vanilla extract.

Foaming Sauce

1 cup butter or oleo
2 cups confectioners' sugar
2 egg whites
5 tablespoons of wine or 3 of brandy
¼ cup boiling water

Beat butter to a cream, gradually add sugar. Add egg whites unbeaten, one at a time, then brandy or wine. When all is a light smooth mass, add water slowly beating meanwhile. Place the bowl in a basin of hot water and stir until foamy or about 2 minutes.

Quick Raspberry Cream Sauce

2/3 cup sweetened condensed milk
¼ cup lemon juice
1 teaspoon grated lemon rind

¼ cup hot water
½ cup fresh raspberries

Blend thoroughly condensed milk, lemon juice and rind. Stir without cooking until the mixture thickens. Add the hot water, again blending thoroughly. Fold in the raspberries. Serve with cottage pudding or pieces of angel cake.

Cream Sauce

1 cup powdered sugar
½ cup butter

½ cup rich cream

Beat butter and sugar thoroughly, add cream, stir the whole into ½ cup boiling water, place on stove for a few moments, stirring it constantly; take off, and add flavoring of ½ teaspoon vanilla.

Vinegar Sauce

1 tablespoon butter
1 tablespoon flour
¼ cup vinegar
½ cup molasses or brown sugar
1 cup cold water
½ cup sugar
¼ teaspoon nutmeg

Mix above ingredients together and stir until it boils. Serve hot.

Molasses Sauce

1 cup molasses
½ cup warm water
1 tablespoon of butter
½ teaspoon cinnamon
¼ teaspoon salt
3 tablespoons vinegar

Boil together for 20 minutes. The juice of a lemon can be used instead of vinegar. This sauce is nice for apple or rice puddings.

Rich Wine Sauce

1 cup butter or oleo   ½ cup wine, Madeira, Port or Tokay
2 cups confectioners' sugar

Beat butter to a cream. Add the sugar gradually, when very light add the wine, heated, a little at a time. Place the bowl in a basin of hot water and stir for two minutes. This sauce should be smooth and foamy.

Brown Sauce

2 tablespoons butter or fat
2 tablespoons flour
1 cup hot water or fish stock
½ teaspoon salt
⅛ teaspoon pepper

Brown the butter or fat, add a small onion chopped if desired. Add the flour, allow to brown and then gradually add the hot liquid to the seasoning.

Egg Sauce

2 yolks of eggs
1 tablespoon lemon juice or vinegar
1 cup brown sauce (see recipe above)

Beat the yolks and gradually stir the hot brown sauce in them. Allow to cook for a moment, stirring constantly until thick. Remove from fire and add lemon juice.

Drawn Butter

1/3 cup butter   ⅛ teaspoon pepper
3 tablespoons flour   ½ teaspoon salt
1½ cups hot water

Melt half the butter, add flour mixed with seasoning and then gradually add hot water. Boil 5 minutes and add remaining butter piece by piece.

Cocktail Sauce

6 tablespoons tomato catsup   4 tablespoons lemon juice
2 tablespoons horseradish   Celery salt and Tobasco sauce to taste

Shake the ingredients in a jar or wide-mouthed bottle until well mixed.

Hollandaise Sauce

½ cup butter   3 egg yolks
3 tablespoons flour   Lemon juice to taste
1 pint boiling water

Melt half the butter and sift in flour. Stir and cook, slowly adding pint of boiling water, beating until smooth. Add the butter, a small piece at a time, stirring each piece in thoroughly before adding the next, until all the butter is mixed in. Draw aside from the fire and add the beaten egg yolks, keeping the mixture just under the boiling point, beating the sauce as it thickens. Do not allow it to boil any more or the sauce will curdle. Add lemon juice to taste. Sauce should be thick, yellow like a custard, and slightly acid.

Lobster Sauce

3 tablespoons butter   ⅛ teaspoon pepper
3 tablespoons flour   1 cup milk
1 teaspoon salt   ½ cup cream
1 to 1½ cups freshly cooked lobster

Melt butter, add flour and seasonings and stir steadily until blended. Pour in gradually milk and cream, and simmer for 2 minutes. Add chunks of freshly cooked lobster. Heat through, not boiling.

Port Wine Sauce

½ tumbler currant jelly   2 tablespoons lemon juice
½ tumbler port wine   4 cloves
½ tumbler stock   Dash of cayenne
½ teaspoon salt

Simmer cloves in stock for ½ hour — strain onto other ingredients and let all melt together. Part of the gravy from the game may be added to it. Nice on goose, duck or venison and rabbit.

Egg Sauce

4 tablespoons butter   ½ teaspoon salt
4 tablespoons flour   ⅛ teaspoon pepper
2 cups hot milk   2 hard-cooked eggs

Melt butter, add flour and blend well. Add hot milk and cook until thick. Slice hard-cooked eggs and add to sauce. Serve with boiled fish.

VARIATION: In place of sliced hard-cooked eggs, drop one or two raw eggs in the cooked sauce and when cooked chop egg up in the sauce.

Cheese Sauce

3 tablespoons butter   ½ teaspoon salt
¼ cup flour   Cayenne pepper
1½ cups hot milk   6 ounces process cheese

Melt the butter in a sauce pan; add the flour and rub to a paste, gradually adding the hot milk; stir and cook until thick; add the salt, a few grains of cayenne pepper; remove from the stove and add the process cheese, which melts without becoming stringy and tough; stir until the mixture is smooth. Serve over fish.

Tartar Sauce

For deep fried fish or pan fried oysters, scallops, etc.

1 cup mayonnaise   1 tablespoon minced capers
1 tablespoon minced pickles 1 tablespoon minced onion
1 tablespoon minced parsley

Mix thoroughly and serve cold.

Currant Jelly Sauce

3 tablespoons butter
1 onion
1 bay leaf
1 sprig celery
2 tablespoons vinegar
½ cup currant jelly
2 cups hot water or stock
1 tablespoon flour
Salt and pepper

Cook butter and onions until faintly browned — add flour and herbs, stir until well browned, add the stock and simmer 20 minutes. Strain, skim fat, add jelly and serve with game.

Currant Sauce

Melt 1 tablespoon currant jelly and 3 tablespoons of butter and beat — serve on venison steaks

Parsley Butter

1 tablespoon butter
1 teaspoon minced parsley
1 teaspoon lemon juice
¼ teaspoon salt
Few grains of pepper

Rub butter until creamy and add other ingredients.

Ginger Lemonade

(Over 100 Years Old)

½ cup vinegar
1 cup sugar
2 teaspoonfuls ginger

Mix together in quart pitcher, fill with ice water. It is a cooling drink and almost as good as lemonade, some preferring it.

Spizzerinktum

2 eggs
½ cup sugar
⅛ teaspoon salt
Juice of 1 lemon
Juice of 3 oranges
2 cups cranberry juice
Cracked ice

Beat eggs, sugar and salt until thick and lemon colored. Add lemon, orange and cranberry juice and blend. Pour over cracked ice in glasses or punch cups. Five 8-ounce glasses.

Sham Champagne

(Over 100 Years Old)

A good temperance drink is made as follows:

1 ounce tartaric acid	1½ cups white sugar
1 lemon	2½ gallons water
½ ounce ginger root	4 ounces brewers yeast

Slice the lemon, bruise the ginger, mix all except yeast. Boil the water and pour it upon them. Let it stand until blood heat, then add yeast, let stand in sun all day, at night bottle. In two days it will be fit for use.

Easter Parade Punch

(Makes 40 Sherbet Cups)

2 quarts lime rickey	1 quart orange juice
1 quart vanilla ice cream	½ cup lemon juice
1 quart orange sherbet	

Juice from 8-ounce bottle of maraschino cherries

Beat all together until well mixed. Add two quarts lime rickey just before serving. Use cherries to garnish.

Sparkling Cranberry Punch

1 quart cranberries	1 cup orange juice
1 quart water	½ cup lemon juice
2 cups sugar	1 pint ginger ale

Cook together cranberries and water — strain through two thicknesses of wet cheesecloth. Add sugar and stir over heat until the sugar is dissolved. Cool and add orange and lemon juice. Pour in the ginger ale and dilute with ice water. Pour over chipped ice and serve.

Grape Juice Cocktail

3 tablespoons lemon juice	1 pint ginger ale
2 cups grape juice	

Have the ingredients thoroughly chilled, shake together like grape juice with the lemon juice, add the ginger ale and serve at once.

Raspberry Punch

(Serves 25)

4 cups sugar
3 cups water
3 dozen lemons
1 dozen oranges
2 quarts crushed raspberries

4 cups diced pineapple and juice
2 quarts tea infusion
½ teaspoon salt
1 quart ginger ale

Boil sugar and water together five to eight minutes and cool. Wash the lemons and oranges, squeeze out the juice. Cover the skins with water and let stand an hour or two, pour off water and add to juice. Mix fruit juice with raspberries and pineapple. Add tea and salt. When ready to serve, add ginger ale and pour over cracked ice. Dilute with ice water if desired.

Lime Julep

½ cup sugar
1 cup water
4 eggs

1 cup lime juice
2 2/3 cups milk

Boil sugar and water together to make a syrup. After it has boiled 10 minutes, add the lime juice. Allow this to cool. Using ¾ cup of the mixture, add the eggs and milk and beat all together with rotary egg beater for several minutes. Divide into 4 glasses. Fill with charged or plain water and serve.

Ginger Beer

(White House Cook Book 1887)

Put into a kettle two ounces of powdered ginger root (or more if it is not very strong), half an ounce of cream of tartar, two large lemons, cut in slices, two pounds of broken loaf sugar and two gallons of soft boiling water. Simmer them over a slow fire for half an hour. When the liquor is nearly cold, stir into it a large tablespoonful of the best yeast. After it has fermented, which will be in about twenty-four hours, bottle for use.

White Spruce Beer

(Over 100 Years Old)

3 pounds loaf sugar
5 gallons water
1 cup good yeast (1 yeast cake)

A small piece lemon peel
Essence of spruce

Mix all together, when fermented preserve in closed bottles. Molasses or brown sugar can be used and the lemon peel left out. If unable to obtain essence of spruce, twigs may be boiled down. This is a delightful home drink.

Peppermint Tea

½ cup sugar
1 cup water
Few grains salt
1/3 cup grapefruit juice

3 tablespoons lemon juice
¼ cup unsweetened pineapple juice
1 cup crushed ice
¼ teaspoon peppermint extract

Heat sugar, water and salt until the sugar is completely dissolved, add the fruit juices, then the crushed ice, and finally the peppermint extract.

When serving, add ice or cold water as desired.

Spiced Tea

(Serves Six)

4 tablespoons lemon juice
Sugar syrup
Mint
6 teaspoons tea

6 cups boiling water
1 teaspoon whole allspice
1 teaspoon whole cloves
1 small piece cinnamon
6 tablespoons orange juice

Pour boiling water over the allspice, cloves and cinnamon. Cover and let boil 3 minutes. Add tea, and let steep about 3 minutes. Strain. Cool and add orange and lemon juice. Sweeten to taste with sugar syrup (equal parts of sugar and water boiled together until syrup forms). Serve in tall glasses with cracked ice. Garnish with a sprig of mint.

Raspberry Shrub

Place red raspberries in a stone jar, cover with good cider vinegar, let stand overnight; next morning strain, and to 1 pint of juice add 1 pint of sugar. Boil 10 minutes and bottle while hot.

Orange Egg Punch

1 egg

1 tablespoon sugar

Few grains salt

¼ cup orange juice

1 cup milk

Beat egg until light and add sugar and salt. Add orange juice, mix thoroughly. Then slowly add the milk. Serve very cold.

Spiced Cider

(Serves 25)

1 gallon cider

1 tablespoon whole cloves

1 tablespoon allspice berries

4 sticks cinnamon (about 2 inches each)

3 lemons (optional)

3 oranges (optional)

Place cider and spices in a kettle, heat slowly, stirring often. Strain. Chill. Add fruit juices to taste, if desired.

Eggnog

2 eggs, separated

¼ cup sugar

¼ teaspoon salt

2 cups milk

1 teaspoon vanilla

I

Add salt to egg whites and beat until foamy. Add sugar gradually, continue beating until shiny and whites form soft peaks when beater is withdrawn. Beat yolks and vanilla until well blended. Fold into egg whites. Add milk. Serve.

II

Using ingredients above, scald milk in double boiler or over low heat. Add sugar and salt to egg yolks. Blend thoroughly. Gradually stir in milk. Cook in double boiler or over low heat stirring constantly until mixture coats spoon. Chill. Fold in stiffly beaten egg whites and vanilla. Serve.

Divinity Fudge

3 cups granulated sugar

½ cup light corn syrup

½ cup cold water

2 egg whites, beaten stiffly (room temperature)

Few grains of salt

1 teaspoon vanilla

½ cup walnuts, cut up

Food coloring if desired

Place sugar, syrup, and water in pan over low heat. Stir only until sugar is dissolved. Cook to 234°F. Pour one-half of syrup mixture slowly in beaten egg whites, beating continually as you pour. Cook remaining syrup to 280°F. Add this syrup slowly to egg mixture, beating constantly. Add vanilla and walnuts. Continue beating until mixture is thick enough to drop from spoon and when dropped on a piece of waxpaper will not lose shape. Pour immediately into a buttered 9 x 9 inch tin. As soon as it sets, cut into squares.

One may also drop the divinity by spoonfuls onto a piece of waxpaper. A little red coloring may be added to half of it to make some pale pink drops with the white drops.

Brown Sugar Fudge

1 cup white sugar

1 cup light brown sugar, packed

2/3 cup milk

Few grains of salt

2 tablespoons butter

1 teaspoon vanilla extract

½ cup nuts (optional)

Place sugars, milk and salt in a saucepan and cook, stirring constantly until fudge boils rapidly. Let boil until temperature reaches 239 degrees or until a firm ball is formed when a few drops are placed in cold water. Remove from heat and follow the very same procedure as in the recipe for making chocolate fudge. When cool, beat and pour into buttered square pan and mark into squares.

Variation: Sour cream fudge is made by the same method, substituting 3 cups brown sugar and 1 cup of sour cream in place of the white and brown sugar and milk.

Old Fashioned White Taffy

1½ cups sugar

½ cup water

½ tablespoon vinegar

¼ teaspoon cream of tartar

1 teaspoon lemon extract

Place the sugar, water, vinegar and cream of tartar in a saucepan. Cook to 290°, or to the soft-crack stage. Add the extract and pour on a buttered platter. When cool enough to handle, pull until white and glossy. Cut into sticks or cushions.

Date and Raisin Slices

This candy is uncooked and improves with age. It is also good for children.

½ cup seeded raisins

¼ cup pitted prunes

1 cup pitted dates

1 teaspoon grated lemon peel

¼ cup granulated sugar

¼ cup finely chopped nuts

1 tablespoon grated orange peel

Combine all fruits by running through food chopper. Add orange and lemon peel and sugar. Form into roll, cover with nut meats. Chill and slice.

Old Fashioned Molasses Taffy

1¼ cups sorghum or dark molasses

¾ cup sugar

1 tablespoon vinegar

1 tablespoon butter

⅛ teaspoon soda

⅛ teapsoon salt

Combine sorghum, sugar and vinegar and cook to 270°, or to the soft-crack stage; stir occasionally to prevent burning. Remove from heat, add butter, soda, and salt, and stir just enough to blend. Pour into buttered pans. When cool enough to handle, gather into a ball and pull between ungreased fingertips until firm and light in color. Cut into pieces and wrap in waxed paper. Add, if desired, a few drops of oil of peppermint or of peppermment extract to the above recipe before pulling.

Rum Balls

2 cups vanilla wafer crumbs
1 cup pecan nuts, chopped
1 cup confectioners' sugar

2 tablespoons cocoa
2 tablespoons white corn syrup
1/3 cup rum or brandy

Roll crumbs fine. Add other ingredients and mix well. Shape by teaspoons into firm balls. Roll in confectioners' sugar or dry cocoa and store tightly for at least one week before using so that flavors will blend. Makes 50.

Vinegar Candy

2½ cups sugar
2 tablespoons molasses
2 tablespoons vinegar

1/3 cup water
Butter size of two walnuts
Peanuts

Mix ingredients, except the peanuts, and boil until it forms a soft ball in water. Remove. Set it in pan of cold water and beat until cool. Add peanuts. (Important to wait until cool before adding nuts.) Continue to beat until the glossy look leaves. Spread quickly in a warm, buttered cookie pan. Let set. Break off in chunks. Delicious and different.

Submitted by Mrs. Esther Dolliver, Owls Head, Maine

Popcorn Balls or Squares

1 cup molasses
½ cup sugar
½ teaspoon salt

1 tablespoon butter
2 quarts popcorn

Combine all four ingredients in saucepan and boil together gently until a small amount tested in cold water forms a firm ball, but not brittle, unless you like your popcorn balls real hard. Pour over 2 quarts of popcorn, blending and stirring — then press down in a shallow pan. When firm, cut in squares; or form popcorn mixture into balls. Peanuts are also good added to the popcorn if it is used for squares.

Chocolate Fudge

2 cups sugar

1½ to 2 squares chocolate

2/3 cup milk

Few grains of salt

2 tablespoons butter

1 teaspoon vanilla extract

½ cup nuts (optional)

Heat milk and chocolate together until chocolate is melted over low heat. Remove from heat as soon as chocolate is melted and beat to smooth consistency. This method prevents curdling. Add to sugar and salt in a saucepan and heat slowly, stirring until sugar is dissolved and fudge begins to boil. Wipe any sugar crystals from sides of pan and let boil without stirring until the temperature reaches 236° or a firm soft ball is formed when a few drops are placed in cold water. Remove from heat, cool by setting saucepan in a pan of cold water. Place butter on top of fudge, without stirring, coat top of fudge with butter to prevent fudge from sugaring on top. Cool to lukewarm, add vanilla and nuts. Beat until creamy and mixture loses its shine. Pour into buttered square pan and mark into squares.

Note: If mixture becomes too stiff to spread, the candy may be kneaded and when smooth roll into an oblong strip and when firm cut in slices.

Peanut Butter Fudge

2 cups white sugar

2/3 cup milk

¼ cup chunk style peanut butter

2 tbsp. butter

1 tsp. vanilla

Salt

Place sugar, milk and a few grains of salt in a saucepan and cook, stirring constantly until it boils rapidly. Cook to 236° F. following chocolate fudge directions. When lukewarm, add peanut butter and vanilla and beat until mixture loses its shine. Pour quickly in a buttered tin and mark into squares.

THE
Accomplisht Cook,

O R,

The whole Art and Mystery of

COOKERY, fitted for all Degrees and Qualities.

Recipes from 300 years ago are contained in the next 24 pages reproduced photographically without change from "The Accomplished Cook: Or, The Art and Mystery of Cookery", first published in Leicestershire September 29, 1664.

It is believed that the volume was rewritten and recipes common to the New World added by a printer in Cornhill in Boston sometime prior to 1712. This is substantiated by the inclusion of dishes and ingredients native to the area which is now Massachusetts and Maine.

The fly leaf contains the inscription, "Elis a. Bull   Her Book 1727". Elizabeth Bull was the wife of the first minister to serve Kings Chapel in Boston.

The volume was passed down through the generations of the family to Fannie Weston, wife of Samuel Weston, one time head-master of the Roxbury Latin School in Boston. The book continued through the family to the present owner, Ralph W. Bartlett of Bremen, Maine, who kindly loaned it in order that the many recipes for very early New England cooking it contains might be made available to the public.

In reading the recipes it is well to keep in mind that the letter S appears as f. The quantities are for the large and hearty families of those days. An accomplished cook can reduce them to her needs.

Some of the recipes obviously do not apply to today, but have been included to show the problems confronting the cooks of 300 years ago. Examples are: "To keep lobster a quarter year very good." Others are those relating to the treatment of tainted venison which are unnecessary with today's refrigeration; and are not recommended. They are merely to point out the problems of three centuries ago.

To bake Oysters.

Parboil your oysters in their own liquor, then take them out and wash them in warm water from the dregs, dry them and season them with pepper, nutmeg, yolks of hard eggs, and salt; the pye being made, put a few currans in the bottom, and lay on the oysters, with some slic't dates in halves, some large mace, slic't lemon, barberries, and butter, close it up and bake it, then liquor it with white wine, sugar, and butter; or in place of white wine use ver-juyce.

The Forms of Oyster Pyes.

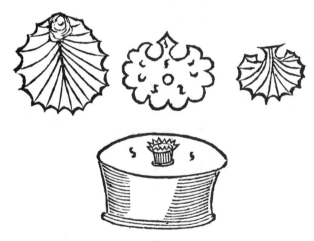

To bake Oysters otherwayes.

Season them with pepper, salt, and nutmegs, the same quantity as beforesaid, and the same quantity of oysters, two or three whole onions, neither currans nor sugar, but add to it in all respects else; as slic't nutmeg on them, large mace, hard eggs in halves, barberries, and butter, liquor it with beaten nutmeg, white wine, and juyce of oranges.

Other-

To fry Oysters.

Take two quarts of great oysters being parboild in their own liquor, and washed in warm water, bread them, dry them, and flour them, fry them in clarified butter crisp and white, then have butter'd prawns or shrimps, butter'd with cream and sweet butter, lay them in the bottom of a clean dish, and lay the fried oysters round about them, run them over with beaten butter, juyce of oranges, bay-leaves stuck round the oysters, and slices of oranges or lemons.

To fry Lobsters.

Being boild take the meat out of the shells, and slice it long wayes, flour it, and fry it in clarified butter, fine, white, and crisp; or in place of flouring it in batter, with eggs, flour, salt, and cream, roul them in it and fry them, being fryed make a sauce with the juyce of oranges, claret wine, and grated nutmeg, beaten up thick with some good sweet butter, then warm the dish and rub it with a clove of garlick, dish the lobsters, garnish it with slices of oranges or lemons, and pour on the sauce.

To stew Lobsters

Take the meat out of the shells, slice it, and fry it in clarified butter, (the lobsters being first boild and cold) then put the meat in a pipkin with some claret wine, some good sweet butter, grated nutmeg, salt, and two or three slices of an orange, let it stew leasurely half an hour, and dish it up on fine carved sippets in a clean dish, with sliced orange on it, and the juyce of another, and run it over with beaten butter.

To hash Lobsters

Take them out of the shells, mince them small, and put them in a pipkin with some claret wine, salt, sweet butter, grated nutmeg, slic't oranges, and some pistaches ; being finely

finely ſtewed, ſerve them on ſippets, diſh them, and run them over with beaten butter, ſlic't oranges, ſome cuts of paſte, or lozenges of puff-paſte.

To boil Lobſters to eat cold the common way.

Take them alive or dead, lay them in cold water to make the claws ruff, and keep them from breaking off; then have a kettle over the fire with fair water, put in it as much bay ſalt as will make it a good ſtrong brine, when it boils ſcum it, and put in the lobſters, let them boil leaſurely the ſpace of half an hour or more, according to the bigneſs of them, being well boild take them up, weſh them, and then wipe them with beer and butter, and keep them for your uſe.

To keep Lobſters a quarter of a year very good.

Take them being boild as aforeſaid wrap them in courſe rags having been ſteeped in brine, and bury them in a cellar in ſome ſea-ſand pretty deep.

To farce a Lobſter.

Take a lobſter being half boild, take the meat out of the ſhells, and mince it ſmall with a good freſh eel, ſeaſon it with cloves and mace beaten, ſome ſweet herbs minced ſmall and mingled amongſt the meat, yolks of eggs gooſeberries, grapes, or barberries, and ſometimes boild artichocks cut into dice-work, or boild aſparagus, and ſome almond paſte mingled with the reſt, fill the lobſters ſhells, claws, tail, and body, and bake it in a blote oven, make ſauce with the gravy and white-wine, and beat up the ſauce or lear with good ſweet butter, a grated nutmeg, juyce of oranges, and an anchove, and rub the diſh with a clove of garlick.

To this farcing you may ſometimes add almond paſte,

currans, sugar, gooseberries, and make balls to lay about the lobsters, or serve it with venison sauce.

To *marinate Lobsters.*

Take lobsters out of the shells being half boild, then take the tails and lard them with a salt eel, (or not lard them) part the tails into two halves the longest way, and fry them in sweet sallet oyl, or clarified butter; being finely fryed, put them into a dish or pipkin, and set them by; then make sauce with white-wine, and white wine vinegar, four or five blades of large mace, three or four slic't nutmegs, two races of ginger slic't, some ten or twelve cloves, twice as much of whole pepper, and some salt, boil them altogether with rosemary, tyme, winter savory, sweet marjoram, bay-leaves, sage, and parsley, the tops of all these herbs about an inch long ; then take three or four lemons and slice them, dish up the lobsters on a clean dish, and pour the broth, herbs, and spices on the fish, lay on the lemons, run it over with some of the oyl or butter they were fryed in, and serve them up hot.

To *broil Lobsters.*

Being boild lay them on a gridiron, or toast them against the fire, and baste them with vinegar and butter, or butter only, broil them leasurely, and being broild serve them with butter and vinegar beat up thick with slic't lemon and nutmeg.

Otherwayes.

Broil them, the tails being parted in two halves long wayes, also the claws cracked and broild, broil the barrel whole being salted, baste it with sweet herbs, as tyme, rosemary, parsley, and savory, being broild dish it, and serve it with butter and vinegar.

To bake Lobsters to be eaten hot.

Being boild and cold, take the meat out of the shells,
and season it lightly with nutmeg, pepper, salt, cinamon,
and ginger; then lay it in a pie made according to the
following form, and lay on it some dates in halves, large
mace, sliced lemons, barberries, yolks of hard eggs and
butter, close it up and bake it, and being baked liquor it
with white-wine, butter, and sugar, and ice it. On flesh
dayes put marrow to it.

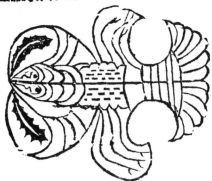

Otherwayes.

Take the meat out of the shells being boild and cold,
and lard it with a salt eel or salt salmon, seasoning it with
beaten nutmeg, pepper, and salt; then make the pie,
put some butter in the bottom, and lay on it some slices of a fresh eel, and on that a layer of lobsters, put to
it a few whole cloves, and thus make two or three layers, last of all slices of fresh eel, some whole cloves and
butter, close up the pie, and being baked, fill it up with
clarified butter.

If you bake it this wayes to eat hot, season it lightly,
and put in some large mace; liquor it with claret-wine,
beaten butter, and slices of orange.

To broil Lobsters on paper.

Slice the tails round, and also the claws in long slices, then butter a dripping-pan made of paper, lay it on a gridiron, and put some slices of lobster seasoned with nutmeg and salt, and slices of a fresh eel some sage leaves, tops of rosemary, two or three cloves, and sometimes some bay leaves or sweet herbs chopped; broil them on the embers, and being finely broild serve them on a dish and a plate in the same dripping-pan, put to them beaten butter, juyce of oranges, and slices of lemon.

To roast Lobsters.

Take a lobster, and spit it raw on a small spit, binde the claws and tail with packthred, baste it with butter, vinegar, and sprigs of rosemary, and salt it in the roasting.

Otherwayes.

Half boil them, take them out of the shells, and lard them with small lard made of a salt eel, lard the claws and tails, and spit the meat on a small spit, with some slices of the eel, and sage or bay-leaves between, stick in the fish here and there a clove or two, and some sprigs of rosemary; roast the barrel of the lobster whole, and baste them with sweet butter: make sauce with claret wine, the gravy of the lobsters, juyce of oranges, an anchove or two, and sweet butter beat up thick with the core of a lemon, and grated nutmeg.

To broil Crabs in Oyl or Butter.

Take crabs being boild in water and salt, steep them in oyl and vinegar, and broil them on a gridiron on a soft fire of embers, in the broiling baste them with some rosemary branches, and being broild serve them with the sauces they were broild with, oyl and vinegar, or beaten butter, vinegar, and the rosemary branches they were basted with

To fry Crabs.

Take the meat out of the great claws being first boild, flour and fry them, and take the meat out of the body, strain half of it for sauce, and the other half to fry, and mix it with grated bread, almond paste, nutmeg, salt, and yolks of eggs, fry it in clarified butter, being first dipped in batter, put in a spoonful at a time; then make sauce with wine-vinegar, butter, or juyce of orange, and grated nutmeg, beat up the butter thick, and put some of the meat that was strained into the sauce, warm it and put it in a clean dish, lay the meat on the sauce, slices of orange over all, and run it over with beaten butter, fryed parsley round the dish brim, and the little legs round the meat.

To bake Crabs in Pye, Dish, or Patty-pan.

Take four or five crabs being boild, take the meat out of the shells and claws as whole as you can, season it with nutmeg and salt lightly; then strain the meat that came out of the body-shells with a little claret-wine, some cinamon, ginger, juyce of orange and butter, make the pie, dish, or patty-pan, lay butter in the bottom, then the meat of the claws, some pistaches, asparagus, some bottoms of artichocks, yolks of hard eggs, large mace, grapes, gooseberries or barberries, dates of slic't orange, and butter, close it up and bake it, being baked, liquor it with the meat out of the body.

To fry *Muskles*.

Take as much water as will cover them, set it a boiling, and when it boils put in the muskles, being clean washed, put some salt to them, and being boild take them out of the shells, and beard them from the stones, moss, and gravel, wash them in warm water, wipe them dry, flour them, and fry them crisp, serve them with beaten butter, juyce of orange, and fryed parsley, or fryed sage dipped in batter, fryed ellicksander leaves, and slic't orange.

To make a *Muskle* Pye.

Take a peck of muskles, wash them clean, and set them a boiling in a kettle of fair water, (but first let the water boil)then put them into it, give them a walm, and as soon as they are opened, take them out of the shells, stone them, and mince them with some sweet herbs, some leeks, pepper, and nutmeg ; mince six hard eggs and put to them, put some butter in the pye, close it up and bake it, being baked liquor it with some butter, white-wine, and slices of orange.

To stew Prawns, Shrimps, or Craw-fish.

Being boild and picked, stew them in white-wine, sweet butter, nutmeg, and salt, dish them in scollop shells, and run them over with beaten butter, and juyce of orange or lemon.

Otherwayes, stew them in butter and cream, and serve them in scollop-shells.

To stew Lobsters.

Take claret-wine, vinegar, nutmeg, salt, and butter stew them down somewhat dry, and dish them in a scollop shell, run them over with butter and slic't lemon.

To broil or toast Salmon.

Take a whole salmon, a jole, rand, chine, or slices cut round it the thickness of an inch, steep these in wine vinegar, good sweet sallet oyl and salt, broil them on a soft fire, and baste them with the same sauce they were steeped in, with some streight sprigs of rosemary, sweet marjoram, tyme, and parsley ; the fish being broild, boil up the gravy and oyster liquor, dish up the fish, pour on the sauce, and lay the herbs about it.

To roast a Salmon according to this Form.

Take a salmon, draw it at the gills, and put in some sweet herbs in his belly whole ; the salmon being scaled and the slime wiped off, lard it with pickled herrings, or a fat salt eel, fill his belly with some great oysters stewed, and some nutmeg ; let the herbs be tyme, rosemary, winter savory, sweet marjoram, a little onion and garlick, put them in the belly of the salmon, baste it with butter, and set it in an oven in a latten dripping-pan, lay it on sticks and baste it with butter, draw it, turn it, and put some claret wine in the pan under it, let the gravy drip into it, baste it out of the pan with rosemary and bayes, and put some anchoves into the wine also, with some pepper and nutmeg ; then take the gravy and clear off the fat, boil it up, and beat it thick with butter ; then put the fish in a large dish, pour the sauce on it, and rip up his belly, take out some of the oysters, and put them in the sauce, and take away the herbs.

Section 5.

The best way of making all manner of Sallets.

To make a grand Sallet of divers Compounds.

TAke a cold roast capon and cut it into thin slices square and small, (or any other roast meat, as chicken, mutton, veal, or neats tongue) mingle with it a little minced taragon and an onion; then mince lettice as small as the capon, mingle all together, and lay it in the middle of a clean scowred dish. Then lay capers by themselves, olives by themselves, samphire by it self, broom-buds, pickled mushrooms, pickled oysters, lemon, orange, raisins, almonds, blew figs, Virginia Potato, caperons, crucifex pease, and the like, more or less, as occasion serves, lay them by themselves in the dish round the meat in partitions. Then garnish the dish sides with quarters of oranges and lemons, or in slics, oyl and vinegar beaten together, and poured on it over all

On fish days, a roast, broild, or boild pike, boned, and being cold, slice it as abovesaid.

Another way for a grand Sallet.

Take the buds of all good sallet herbs, capers, dates, raisins, almonds, currans, figs, orangado. Then first of all lay it in a large dish, the herbs being finely picked and

wafhed, fwing them in a clean napkin; then lay the other
mater as round the dfh, and amongft the herbs fome of
all the forefaid fruits, fome fine fugar, and on the top flic't
lemon, and eggs fcarce hard cut in halves, and laid round
the fide of the cifh, and fcrape fugar over all ; or you may
lay every fruit in partitions feveral.

Otherwayes.

Difh firft round the center flic't figs, then currans, capers, almonds, and raifins together ; next beyond that,
olives, beets, cabbidge-lettice, cucumbers, or flic't lemon
carved ; then oyl and vinegar beaten together, the beft oyl
you can get, and fugar or none, as you pleafe ; garnifh the
brims of the difh with orangado, flic't lemon jagged, o-
lives ftuck with flic't almonds, fugar, or none.

Another grand Sallet.

Take all manner of knots of buds of fallet herbs, buds
of pot-herbs, or any green herbs, as fage, mint, balm, bur-
net, violet-leaves, red coleworts ftreaked of divers fine colours, lettice, any flowers, blanched almonds, blue figs, raifins of the fun, currans, capers, olives ; then difh the fallet
in a heap or pile, being mixt with fome of the fruits, and
all finely wafhed and fwung in a napkin, then about the
center lay firft flic't figs, next capers and currans, then almonds and raifins, next olives, and laftly either jagged
beets, jagged lemons, jagged cucumbers, or cabbidge-lettice in quarters, good oyl and wine vinegar, fugar or none.

Otherways.

The youngeft and fmalleft leaves of fpinage, the fmalleft
alfo of forrel, well wafhed currans, and red beets round the
center being finely carved, oyl and vinegar, and the difh
garnifhed with lemon and beets.

Section 21.

The exactest Way for the Dreſſing of Eggs.

To make Omlets divers wayes.

The firſt way.

BReak ſix, eight, or ten eggs more or leſs, beat them together in a diſh, and put ſalt to them ; then put ſome butter a melting in a frying-pan, and fry it more or leſs according to your diſcretion, only on one ſide or bottom.

You may ſometimes make it green with juyce of ſpinage and ſorrel beat with the eggs, or ſerve it with green ſauce, a little vinegar and ſugar boild together, and ſerved up in a diſh with the omlet.

The ſecond way.

Take twelve eggs, and put to them ſome grated white bread finely ſearſed, parſley minced very ſmall, ſome ſugar beaten fine, and fry it well on both ſides.

The third way.

Fry toaſts of manchet, and put the eggs to them being beaten and ſeaſoned with ſalt, and ſome fryed ; pour the butter and fryed parſley over all.

The fourth way.

Take three or four pippins, cut them in round slices, and fry them with a quarter of a pound of butter, when the apples are fryed, pour on them six or seven eggs beaten with a little salt, and being finely fried dish it on a plate-dish, or dish, and strow on sugar.

The fifth way.

Mix with the eggs pine-kernels, currans, and pieces of preserved lemons; being fried roul it up like a pudding, and sprinkle it with rose-water, cinamon-water, and strow on fine sugar.

The sixth way.

Beat the eggs, and put to them a little cream, a little grated bread, a little preserved lemon-peel minced or grated very small, and use it as the former.

The seventh way.

Take a quarter of a pound of interlarded bacon, take it from the rinde, cut it into dice-work, fry it, and being fried, put in some seven or eight beaten eggs with some salt, fry them, and serve them with some grape-verjuyce.

The eighth way.

With minced bacon among the eggs fied and beaten together, or with thin slices of interlarded bacon, and fryed slices of bread.

Eggs otherwayes.

Fry them whole in clarified butter with sprigs of rosmary under, fry them not too hard, and serve them with fried parsley on them, vinegar, butter, and pepper.

To make all manner of Hashes.

First, of Raw beef.

MInce it very small with some beef-suet or lard, some sweet-herbs, pepper, salt, some cloves and mace, blanched chesnuts, or almonds blanched, and put in whole, some nutmeg, and a whole onion or two, and stew it finely in a pipkin with some strong broth the space of two hours; put a little claret to it, and serve it on sippets finely carved, with some grapes or lemon in it also, or barberries, and blow off the fat.

Otherwayes.

Stew beef in gobbets, and cut some fat and lean together as big as a good pullets egg, and put them into a pot or pipkin with some Carrots cut in pieces as big as a walnut, some whole onions, some parsnips, large mace, a faggot of sweet herbs, salt pepper, cloves, and as much water and wine as will cover them, and stew it the space of three hours.

2. *Beef hashed otherways, of the Buttock.*

Cut it into thin slices, and hack them with the back of your knife, then fry them with sweet butter; and being fried, put them in a pipkin with some claret, strong broth, or gravy, cloves, mace, pepper, salt, and sweet butter; being tender stewed the space of an hour, serve them on fine sippets, with slic't lemon, goosberries, barberries, or grapes, and some beaten butter.

3. *Beef hashed otherwayes.*

Cut some buttock-beef into fine thin slices, and half as many slices of fine interlarded bacon, stew it very well and tender with some claret and strong broth, cloves, mace, pepper, and salt; being tender stewed the space of two hours, serve them on fine carved sippets, &c.

To bake a side or half Hanch to be eaten hot.

Take a side of a buck being boned, and the skins taken away, feafon it only with two ounces of peppe , and as much falt, or half an ounce more, lay it on a fheet of fine paſte with two pound of beef-fuet finely minced and beat with a little fair water, and laid under it, clofe it up and bake it, and being fine and tender baked, put to it a good ladle full of gravy, or good ftrong mutton broth.

To make a Paſte for it.

Take a peck of flour by weight, and lay it on the paſte-ry board, make a hole in the midſt of the flour, and put to it five pound of good frefh butter, the yolks of fix eggs and but four whi es, work up the butter and eggs into the flour, and being well wrought together put fome fair water to it, and make it into a ſtiff paſte.

In this fafhion of fallow deer you may bake goat, doe, or a pafty of venifon.

To make meer fauce, or a Pickle to keep Venifon in that is tainted.

Take ftrong, ale and as much vinegar as will make it fharp, boyl it with fome bay falt, and make a ſtrong brine, fcum it and let it ſtand till it be cold, then put in your venifon twelve hours prefs it, parboil it, and feafon it, then bake it as before is fhown.

Other Sauce for tainted Venifon.

Take your venifon, and boil water, beer, and wine. vinegar together and fome bay leaves, tyme, favory rofemary, and fennil, of each a handful, when it boils put in your venifon, parboil it well and prefs it, and feafon it as aforesaid, bake it for to be eaten cold or hot, and put some raw minced mutton under it.

Otherwayes to preserve tainted Venison.

Bury it in the ground in a clean cloth a whole night, and it will take away the corruption, savour, or stink.

Other meer Sauce to counterfeit Beef or Mutton to give it a Venison colour.

Take small beer and vinegar, and parboil your beef in it, let it steep all night, then put some turnsole to it, and being baked, a good judgement shall not discern it from red or fallow deer.

Otherways to counterfeit Ram, Weather, or any Mutton for Venison.

Bloody it in sheeps, lambs, or pigs blood, or any good and new blood, season it as before, and bake it either for hot or cold. In this fashion you may bake mutton, lamb, or kid.

To make Umble Pies.

Lay minced beef suet in the bottom of the pye, or slices of interlarded bacon, and the umbles cut as big as small dice, with some bacon cut in the same form, and seasoned with nutmeg, pepper, and salt, fill your pyes with it, and slices of bacon and butter, close it up and bake it, and liquor it with claret, butter, and stripped tyme.

To roast Woodcocks in the English Fashion.

First pull and draw them, then being washt and trust, roast them, baste them with butter, and save the gravy, then broil toastes and butter them; being rosted, bread them with bread and flower, and serve them in a clean dish on the toste and gravy.

To boil a Capon or Chicken with Rice.

Boil the capon in fair water and falt, then take half a pound of rice and boil it in milk; being half boiled, put away the milk, and boil it in two quarts of cream, put to it a little rofe water, and large mace, or nutmeg, with the forefaid materials. Being almoft boil'd, ftrain the yolks of fix or feven eggs with a little cream, and ftir altogether; give them a walm, and difh up the capon or chicken, then pour on the rice, being feafoned with fugar and falt and ferve it on fine carved fippets. Garnifh the difh with fcraped fugar, orange, preferved barberries, flic't lemon, or pomegranate kernels, as alfo the Capon or chicken, and marrow on them.

Divers Meats boiled with Bacon hot or cold; as Calves-head, any Joynt of Veal, lean Venifon, Rabits, Turkey, Peacock, Capons, Pullets, Pheafants, Pewets, Pigeons, Partridges, Ducks, Mallards, or any Sea Fowl.

Take a leg of veal and foak it in fair water, the blood being well foaked from it, and white, boil it, but firft ftuff it with parfley and other fweet herbs chopped fmall, as alfo fome yolks of hard eggs minced; ftuff it and boil it in water and falt, then boil the bacon by its felf either ftuff'd or not, as you pleafe; the veal and bacon being boiled white, being difhed ferve them up, and lay the bacon by the veal with the rinde on in a whole piece, or take off the rinde and cut it in four, fix, or eight thin flices; let your bacon be of the ribs, and ferve it with parfley ftrowed on it, green fauce in faucers, or others, as you may fee in the Book of Sauces.

Several Sauces belonging to Rabits.

1. Beaten butter, and rub the difh with a clove of garlick.

2. Sage and parsley minced, roul it in a ball with some butter, and fill the belly with this stuffing:

To roast a Hen or Pullet.

Take a Pullet or Hen full of egg, draw it and roast it; being roasted break it up, and mince the brauns in thin flices, save the wings whole, or not mince the brauns, and leave the rump with the legs whole; stew all in the gravy and a little salt.

Then have a minced lemon, and put it into the gravy, dish the minced meat in the midst of the dish, and the thighs, wings, and rumps about it. Garnish the dish with oranges and lemon quartered, and serve them up covered.

Sauce with Oysters and Bacon.

Take oysters being parboild and clenged from the grunds, mingle them with pepper, salt, beaten nutmeg, time and sweet marjoram, fill the pullets belly, and roast it, as also two or three ribs of interlarded bacon, serve it in two pieces in the dish with the pullet; then make sauce of the gravy, some of the oyster liquor, oysters and juyce of oranges boild together, take some of the oysters out of the pullets belly, and lay on the breast of it, then put the sauce to it with slices of lemon.

Sauce for Hens or Pullets to prepare them to roast.

Take a pullet or hen, if lean, lard it, if fat, not; or lard ei her fat or lean with a piece or slice of bacon over it, and a piece of interlarded bacon in the belly, seasoned with nutmeg and pepper, and stuck with cloves.

Then for the sauce take the yolks of six hard eggs minced small, put to them white-wine or wine-vinegar, butter, and the gravy of the hen, juyce of orange, pepper, salt, and if you please add thereto mustard.

Section II.

To make all manner of made Dishes, with, or without Paste.

To make a Paste for a Pye.

TAke to a gallon of flour a pound of butter, boil it in fair water, and make the paste up quick.

To make cool Butter Paste for Patty pans or Pasties.

Take to every peck of flour five pound of butter, the whites of six eggs, and work it well together with cold spring water ; you must bestow a great deal of pains, and but little water, or you put out the millers eyes. This paste is good only for patty-pan and pasty.

Sometimes for this paste put in but eight yolks of eggs, and but two whites, and six pound of butter.

To make Paste for thin bake't Meats.

The paste for your thin and standing bake't meats must be made with boiling water, then put to every peck of flour two pound of butter, but let your butter boil first in your liquor.

To make Custard Paste.

Let it be only boiling water and flour without butter, or put sugar to it, which will add to the stiffness of it, and together very well and ftiff, then roul it out very thin, and put flour under it and over it, then take near a pound of butter, and lay it in bits all over it, double it in five or fix doubles; this being done, roul it out the fecond time, and ferve it as at the firft, then roul it out and cut it into what form, or for what ufe you pleafe; you need not fear the curle, for it will divide as often as you double it, which ten or twelve times is enough for any ufe.

The fecond way.

Take a quart of flour, and a pound and a half of butter, work the half pound of butter dry into the flour, then put three or four eggs to it, and as much cold water as will make it leith pafte, work it in a piece of a foot long, then ftrew a little flour on the table, take it by the end, and beat it till it ftretch to be long, then put the ends together, and beat it again, and fo do five or fix times, then work it up round, and roul it up broad; then beat your pound of butter with a rouling-pin, that it may be little, take little bits of thereof, and ftick it all over the pafte, fold up your pafte clofe, and coaft it down with your rouling-pin, roul it out again, and fo do five or fix times, then ufe it as you will.

The third way.

Break two eggs into three pints of flour, make it with cold water, and roul it out pretty thick and fquare, then take fo much butter as pafte, lay it in ranks, and divide your butter in five pieces, that you may lay it on at five feveral times, roul your pafte very broad, and ftick one part of the butter in little pieces all over your pafte, then throw a handful of flour flightly on, fold up your pafte, and beat it with a rowling-pin, fo roul it out again, thus do five times, and make it up.

To make an Almond Tart.

Strain beaten almonds with cream, yolks of eggs, sugar, cinamon, and ginger, boil it thick, and fill your tart, being baked ice it.

To make a Damsin Tart.

Boil them in wine, and strain them with cream, sugar, cinamon, and ginger, boil it thick and fill your tart.

To make a Spinage Tart of three colours, green, yellow and white.

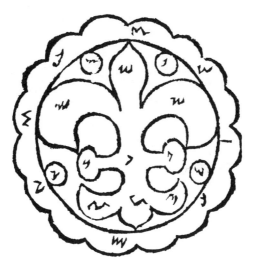

Take two handfuls of young tender spinage, wash it and put it into a skillet of boiling liquor; being tender boild have a quart of cream boild with some whole cinamon, quartered nutmeg, and a grain of musk; then strain the cream, twelve yolks of eggs, and the boild spinage into a dish, with some rose-water, a little sack, and some fine sugar, boil it over a chafing-dish of coals, and stir it that it curd not, keep it till the tart be dried in the oven, and dish it in the form of three colours, green, white, and yellow.

To make Cream Tarts.

Thicken cream with muskefied bisket bread, and serve it in a dish, stick wafers round about it, and slices of

preserved citteron, and in the middle a preserved orange with biskets, the garnish of the dish being of puff-paste.

Or you may boil quin- ces, wardens, pears, and pippins in slices or quarters, and strain them into cream, as also these fruits, melacattons, necturnes, apricocks, peaches, plums, or cherries, and make your tarts of these forms.

To make a French Tart.

Take a pound of almonds, blanch and beat them into fine paste in a stone mortar, with rose-water, then beat the white breast of a cold roste turkey being minced, and beat with it a pound of lard minced, with the marrow of four bones, and a pound of butter, the juyce of three le- mons, two pound of hard sugar; being fine beaten, slice a whole green piece of citron in small slices, a quarter of a pound of pistaches, and the yolks of eight or ten eggs, mingle all together, then make a paste for it with cold butter, two or three eggs, and cold water, &c.

To *make a Rice Pudding to bake.*

Boil the rice tender in milk, then season it with nutmeg, mace, rose-water, sugar, yolks of eggs, with half the whites, some grated bread, and marrow minced with ambergreece, and bake it in a buttered dish

To *make Rice Puddings in guts.*

Boil half a pound of rice with three pints of milk, and a little beaten mace, boil it until the rice be dry, but never stir it, if you do, you must stir it continually, or else it will burn; pour your rice into a cullender or strainer, that the moisture may run clean from it, then put to it six eggs, (put away the whites of three) half a pound of suga, a quarter of a pint of rose-water, a pound of currans, and a pound of beef-suet shred small; season it with nutmeg, cinamon, and salt, then dry the small guts of a hog, sheep, or beefer, and being finely cleansed for the purpose, steep and fill them, cut the guts a foot long, and fill them three quarters full, tie both ends together, and put them in boiling water, a quarter of an hour will boil them.

Otherwayes.

Boil the rice first in water, then in milk, after with salt in cream; then take six eggs, grated bread, good store of marrow minced small, some nutmeg, sugar, and salt; fill the guts, put them into a pipkin, and boil them in milk and rose-water.

Otherwayes.

Steep it in fair water all night, then boil it in new milk, and drain out the milk through a cullender, then mince a good quantity of beef-suet not too small, and put it into the rice in some bowl or tray, with currans being first boild, yolks of eggs, nutmeg, cinamon, sugar, and barberries mingled all together; then wash the second guts, fill them and boil them.

To make a Cinamon Pudding.

Take and steep a penny white loaf in a quart of cream, six yolks of eggs, and but two whites, dates, half an ounce of beaten cinamon, and some almond paste. Sometimes add ro e-water, salt, and boild currans, either bake or boil it for stuffings.

To make a Haggas Pudding.

Take a calves chaldron being well scowred or boild, mince it being cold very fine and small, then take four or five eggs, and leave out half the whites, thick cream, grated bread, sugar, salt, currans, rose-water, some beef suet, or marrow, (and if you will) sweet marjoram, time, parsley, and mix all together; then having a sheeps maw ready dressed, put it in and boil it a little.

Otherwayes.

Take good store of parsley, tyme, savory, four or five onions, and sweet marjoram, chop them with some whole oatmeal, then add to them pepper, and salt, and boil them in a napkin, being boild tender, butter it, and serve it on sippets.

To make a Chiveridge Pudding.

Lay the fattest of a hog in fair water and salt to scowre them, then take the longest and fattest gut, and stuff it with nutmeg, sugar, ginger, pepper, and slic't dates, boil them and serve them to the table.

My Recipes

My Recipes

My Recipes

My Recipes

My Recipes

My Recipes